Publications on Russia and Eastern Europe

of the Institute for Comparative and Foreign Area Studies

NUMBER 3

The Spiritual Regulation
of Peter the Great

TRANSLATED AND EDITED BY

Alexander V. Muller

UNIVERSITY OF WASHINGTON PRESS

SEATTLE & LONDON

Library of Congress Cataloging in Publication Data

Russia. Laws, statutes, etc., 1689–1725 (Peter I).
    The spiritual regulation of Peter the Great.

    Translation of Reglament dukhovnoĭ.
    1. Ecclesiastical law—Russia.   I. Muller,
Alexander V., ed.   II. Title.
Law   344'.47'09   72-4590
ISBN 0-295-95237-7

*Publications on Russia and Eastern Europe of the Institute for Compara-
tive and Foreign Area Studies is a continuation of the series formerly entitled Far Eastern and Russian Institute Publications on Russia and
Eastern Europe.*

Acknowledgment

FOREMOST among all works on the Petrine ecclesiastical reform stands P. V. Verkhovskoi's *Uchrezhdenie Dukhovnoi kollegii i Dukhovnyi reglament,* a two-volume study that is unsurpassed in the scope of its historiographical survey, the high level of its commentary, and the meticulous presentation of its extensive source materials. All this Verkhovskoi accomplished in the face of an advancing hostile army, the evacuation of his seat of studies at Warsaw, the loss of all but one copy of his first printed edition before it could ever be circulated, and the subsequent publication by three different printing-houses of a second edition during the critical war year of 1916. Verkhovskoi's *magnum opus* will continue for years to come to constitute the starting point and core reference work for investigators in this area, and generations of students will remain grateful for the dedication and tenacious perseverance of this painstaking historian.

It is a pleasure to acknowledge my gratitude to John Keep, who read much of the translation in its early form and proposed helpful suggestions for improvement; to Imre Boba, who invariably and generously shared of his vast bibliographical expertise; to Donald Treadgold, who offered encouragement and assistance that were indispensable to the advancement of this effort; and to Marc Szeftel, who suggested the specific topic, gave sound scholarly advice, and set the standards for precision that, however short of the mark the final result may be, guided the execution of the work.

Special appreciation is due Georges Florovsky, whose profound understanding of Russian history and abiding enthusiasm combined,

[v]

as they have in so many cases, to spark an interest of which the present translation is but a single outgrowth.

My thanks are extended also to Jean Fisher, who retyped a good portion of the original draft, and especially to Margery Lang of the Institute for Comparative and Foreign Area Studies at the University of Washington, who resolved editorial problems with true professional competence.

The task of rendering the present documents into English was undertaken and completed without reference to the one other full English translation of them, which appeared in the eighteenth century, or to any of the partial translations that have subsequently made their way into print. Only after that part of the project was done were other translations consulted. In this sense, then, this is a "fresh" translation, which also means that whatever errors or shortcomings it has are my responsibility.

Contents

Introduction

I

THE *Spiritual Regulation*,[1] which Tsar Peter I in 1720 "consented to sign . . . with his own hand,"[2] constitutes for the Russian Orthodox church the principal legislative enactment of the Petrine period. It established within the framework of public law, i.e., the division of law relating to the state in its sovereign capacity, as opposed to canon law, the law of the church, the basis for a new relationship between the spiritual and secular powers in Russia. It marked for the Russian church the suspension of the system of patriarchal administration and the beginning of the synodal period, which was to last for nearly two hundred years, coterminous with the era of the Russian Empire, 1721–1917.

The purpose of this introduction to the translation of the *Spiritual Regulation* and the Supplement to the *Spiritual Regulation*[3] is to explain as briefly and clearly as possible the historical background and the intellectual sources of those documents.

No attempt has been made here to assay the effects of Petrine ecclesiastical legislation on the inner life of the church as a *societas perfecta* in its own right.[4] The omission is not intended to slight that aspect of ecclesiastical history, which never ceased to develop largely according to its own principles and goals. Church historians, such as Alexander Schmemann and Anton Kartashev, have pointed to the positive aspects of Russian spiritual life during the synodal period, urging the view that the Russian church after Peter should not be regarded as suffering from degeneration or exhaustion.[5]

The emphasis here, however, is institutional, limited in scope to a consideration of the "church-state complex." The secular origin, political intention, and legislative content of the documents to which this introduction refers logically make it so.

II

The subject of the *Spiritual Regulation* as a legislative enactment was the ecclesiastical administration of the Russian church. Yet the authority by which it came to be enacted was that of the tsar; and the ideology that underlay it derived not from the religion-centered traditions of Muscovite Russia, but the seventeenth-century rationalistic and scientific movement of Western Europe. Consequently the *Spiritual Regulation* was in reality, both as to its origin and inspiration, rather more a secular than an ecclesiastical document, and was, moreover, without institutional precedent in the historical evolution of the Orthodox church.

Of course it is true that the *Spiritual Regulation* was largely the product of the pen of Feofan, bishop of Pskov (from 1725, archbishop of Novgorod); that the leading ecclesiastics of the Russian church affixed their signatures to it; and that the foremost primates of the Eastern Orthodox church registered their approval of its provisions setting up a new form of ecclesiastical administration for the nascent Russian Empire. Yet the secular character of the *Spiritual Regulation* was not essentially diminished by these circumstances surrounding its composition and enactment, which lent to it overtones of ecclesiastical origination and approbation.

For, in the first case, Feofan Prokopovich, consecrated in 1718 to the see of Pskov in keeping with Peter's wishes and over the objections of prominent churchmen who questioned the conformity of his beliefs with Orthodox teachings, was a theologian absorbed in what Georges Florovsky has referred to as "the Protestant scholasticism of the seventeenth century." [6] That absorption planted Prokopovich's written works squarely within the compass of German reformed theology; in them his views on Orthodoxy, including its traditions, practices, and theological formulations, bear the stamp of a detached critic. [7] His political theories were epigonous of the religious-political struggle that originated in Reformation ecclesiology and developed around a progression of issues arising with various ramifications from the medieval concept of a unitary Christian *respublica*. [8] That struggle, as Thomas Maynard Parker interprets it, took shape between those who held that an indissoluble union existed between church and state, and those who were beginning to abandon that position.[9] Feofan Prokopovich was committed to the idea of the absolute state, independent of the church and superior in its authority over it.[10] The temporal prince in such a state was invested with all rights, or full power, over the religious affairs of his land and people.[11]

The second substantiation for the secular character of the *Spiritual Regulation* lies in the fact that the endorsements by the Russian high clergy were given under duress. The clergy were given no choice but to respond affirmatively to a personal decree from the tsar, who made an unequivocal demand that the copy of the *Spiritual Regulation* being forwarded to them by military messenger was "for signature." [12] The intimidating form of the order, with its implicit threat for noncompliance, and the clear expression of the tsar's intention, as indicated by the presence of his signature, which had already been entered on the *Spiritual Regulation,* tested every hierarch to whom the document was given for endorsement. The threat sometimes rose to tangible proportions, beyond the level of mere intimation.[13]

Third, approval was granted to a *fait accompli,* which the patriarchs of the Eastern church, hard-pressed by Turkish domination and relying on the continued material and moral support of the Orthodox Russian tsar, were in an uncomfortable position to contravene.[14]

III

By making the *Spiritual Regulation* legally binding on the church in its internal administration, the state unilaterally asserted its jurisdiction in areas of competence that before had fallen within the purview of the church. It voided the effect of the resolution concerning the division and limits of secular and spiritual authority that had been formulated by a church council in 1667, which stated:

Let the conclusion be acknowledged that the tsar has pre-eminence in secular matters, the patriarch in ecclesiastical, so that in this way forever may be safeguarded whole and unshaken the good order of the ecclesiastical establishment.[15]

Through the enactment of the *Spiritual Regulation,* then, the church was in law deprived of what the council had declared was its proper independent administrative capability. The degree to which that capability had existed in fact prior to the *Spiritual Regulation* is a question that can only be pointed to here. For the church in its historical development had already undergone a diminution of its independence prior to the enactment of the *Spiritual Regulation* and even prior to the start of Peter's reign. This movement had its genesis in the early Muscovite state, when in 1448 the Russian Metropolia became autocephalous. It was thereafter no longer dependent on or governed by the Greek church, whose missionaries had brought Christianity to Kievan Rus' four and a half centuries before, but whose hierarchy had in 1439 declared for union with Rome. The announcement of union at the Council of Ferrara-Florence served as the occasion for the Russian Metropolia, by the authority of a council of Russian bishops and the grand prince of Moscow, to be removed in its administration from the jurisdiction of the patriarch of Constantinople, with his synod, and from the at least nominal jurisdiction of the Byzantine emperor.[16] The Metropolia assumed autonomy in the selection of its presiding bishops, the metropolitans, who were thereafter chosen from among Russian candidates and exercised their authority independent of Constantinople.

While the Russian Metropolia thus became self-governing, it was then faced with the situation in which the chief representative of the church no longer resided outside the boundaries of the Muscovite state and away from the authority of the grand prince of Moscow. With the church now included within the confines of a growing national state, itself to be soon formally freed of the last vestiges of foreign hegemony, the stage was set for a new relationship between the metropolitan, as head of a national church, and the grand prince, as head of a state wholly comprehending an autocephalous ecclesiastical establishment.

The form that the future relationship might take depended, on the one hand, upon the meaning that the grand princes gave to their political sovereignty and, on the other, upon the manner in which the Russian metropolitan and the other Russian bishops responded to the opportunity of developing their own national ecclesiastical creativity and independent action. The conclusion drawn by Nicholas Kapterev is that it was an opportunity forfeited, for the

Russian episcopate possessed neither the strength nor the means for seizing it.[17] The Russian bishops remained largely unread and passive and in the formulation of ecclesiastical policy continued to look elsewhere for direction. They desired to have the support of someone else in the exercise of their episcopal functions and to submit to some other outside leadership.[18]

To what authority that could be relied upon as unquestionably Orthodox could the Russian hierarchs turn in their unwonted independence? This authority soon appeared in the person of the grand prince, later tsar, of Moscow, who assumed the role of guide in the determination of ecclesiastical matters. The rulers of the Muscovite state devoted serious attention to what they regarded as their important responsibility, supervising the currents of church life, directing it in accordance with their judgment, and rendering decisions in matters pertaining to it. The bishops had only to approve and carry out the commands of the secular rulers.[19]

The relationship between the metropolitan and the grand prince that came into being, then, was one in which the former was transformed into a humble servant of the grand prince, fulfilling his commands and desires.[20] When the Russian patriarchate was established in 1589, the added dignity of the office did not automatically reduce its dependence on the secular authority. On the contrary, Kapterev concludes, the patriarch, as the metropolitan before him, depended entirely and in everything on the tsar, who in turn dealt with the patriarch at his discretion, standing on no ceremony with him if he was found to be in any way unsuitable.[21]

It would be an exaggeration, however, to extend this passivity of the Russian hierarchy as a characteristic common to all who held high ecclesiastical posts. Nor would one be justified in inferring from it that church life was totally static. Important and controversial issues were frequently and fiercely debated in church councils, where crucial decisions were made regarding ecclesiastical doctrine, discipline, and reform. Furthermore there were bishops who, as patriarchs, wielded decisive power in the political sphere as well. Still, the individual instances of this dynamic activity in the councils and by leading ecclesiastics occurred irregularly within the manifest hierarchical organization of the church.

If, as traditionally acknowledged, the church be envisaged as a body in which the responsibility for supervision, or oversight, is

vested in the bishops as shepherds of their flocks, to which end they
are granted their episcopal authority by God, then in Muscovite
Rus' the functioning of the episcopate, which assumed as its primary
objective the preservation intact of hallowed piety and belief, tended
to suffer from weakness and lack of initiative. When vital questions
bearing significantly on ecclesiastical and social matters arose in the
councils, they inevitably originated either at the lower levels of the
ecclesiastical structure or at the highest level of the political structure. They were initiated either by elders, monks, or members of the
white (married) clergy or by the sovereign. Seldom did they proceed
from the episcopal milieu.[22]

When a forceful and energetic patriarch appeared, any height-
ened influence exerted by him was largely personal and not directly
attributable to the patriarchal office, so that when the relations between patriarch and tsar vacillated, they did so according to acci-
dents of history and the personalities of the individuals. Those vacil-
lations notwithstanding, the overarching, though tacit, principle of
the relationship remained the same: the dependence of the spiritual
authority on the secular. Not formally expressed, it could nevertheless be inferred from instances of reciprocal action. Without the consent and approval of the secular authority, the patriarchs could not
take a single independent step; much less of course could they do
anything contrary to its wishes and demands.[23] The establishment of
the patriarchate itself in Muscovite Rus' had been accomplished
upon the tsar's initiative.[24] The installation of a patriarch and the
consecration of bishops depended on the selection by the tsar of men
whom he could also trust to be dutiful personal advisors. The large
estates held by Russian bishops tied them into the judicial-administrative service of the state, which carefully exercised its power of appointment in order to control such a potentially strong economic
and social element, whose prestige among the people was considerable.[25] Even after being appointed, bishops were not immune from
inspection and direction. The episcopal administration as a whole,
from the patriarch to the last eparchial bishop, was continually
under the vigilant supervision and control of the tsar,[26] in sharp
contrast to the ideal of a hierarchy pursuing an independent ecclesiastical policy in the manner proclaimed as desirable by the council
of 1667.

Paul Verkhovskoi acknowledges the degree and the kind of dependence by which Kapterev characterizes the Russian church's relationship to the secular authority in Muscovite Rus'.[27] He agrees that the features of that relationship were an understandable and natural consequence of the historical circumstances attending the founding and development of the Russian church.[28] However, he sees nothing untoward in the degree of dependence by the church on the secular power and denies that there was any usurpation of ecclesiastical function or authority by the latter.[29] The position of the church in law was never impinged upon. For, says Verkhovskoi, in the religious environment of the Muscovite state the goals of the spiritual and secular powers were the same.

This "identity of goals" reflected the pervading sense of eschatological direction that had wide currency in Muscovite Rus' through the influence of Orthodox Christian tradition. The ultimate goal in life was conceived to be the salvation of man's immortal soul, and both tsar and patriarch regarded as requisite their participation in the attainment of that goal.[30] If the clergy proved unable to carry out its task, there was no reason, concludes Verkhovskoi, for the tsar not to provide the needed leadership (though he betrays in his closing statement his own misgivings about the tsars' having to assume "the responsibilities of others"[31]).

It is beyond the scope of the present introduction to analyze this issue further: it would require an examination of the religious culture of Muscovite Rus' and the development of the authority of the Muscovite tsars. However, on the basis of Verkhovskoi's conclusion, a question can be posed that bears directly on the eventual impact of the *Spiritual Regulation* on the Russian church: Given the stated condition of ecclesiastical dependence on the secular authority, what may be expected to occur when the goals for the secular and spiritual powers cease to be identical, and when new goals become defined for those powers at the initiative of a historically dominant state? This was the question confronting the Russian church from the middle of the seventeenth century; the issue was brought to a head with Peter's accession.

After 1649 it is possible to speak of something other than *de facto* dependence in Muscovite Rus' of the spiritual on the secular authority, both of whose interests coincide in essence. The term "secularization of the church"[32] can after that time be applied to something other than the fulfillment by the clergy of temporal functions, or the dependence of the bishops on the secular authority in the determination of ecclesiastical matters, or the active interest shown by the grand princes and tsars in such matters. These manifestations of ecclesiastical dependence remained; yet there appeared alongside them a movement whose ideological foundations distinguished it from conditions in the past. From the beginning that movement was marked by a growing divergence of interests along new lines. This was made evident by the emergence of a state increasingly secular in its outlook and divorced from the norms of Orthodox Christian tradition. The state began to formulate new goals for itself in accordance with a new concept of its own authority, an authority envisaged as rooted in the order of creation, in the natural order of human society.[33] In short the state itself was becoming secularized as new normative concepts were accepted that stressed the predominance of the secular authority. That process of secularization expanded in time to include the church, leading to the increased subordination of the spiritual to the secular authority and the regularization of that relationship in secular law.

In the reign of Peter's father, Alexis (1645–76), partial judicial jurisdiction over the clergy was vested in a new agency of the state, the Central Administration of Monasteries,[34] on the basis of provisions contained in the Code of 1649.[35] Although the relationship between the secular and spiritual powers was made no clearer by definitive statement than it had been before, the Code of 1649 did contain differentiation of spheres of authority and ascribed predominance to the secular power in areas of ecclesiastical administration. Against such encroachment expressed in law, Patriarch Nikon (fl. 1652–58) resolved to carry out a realignment of the relationship between patriarch and tsar. Often employing terms strongly redolent of papal claims to superiority over secular princes, Nikon's main purpose was, as Kapterev concludes, to free the ecclesiastical authority from its growing subordination to the secular authority, to make the patriarch independent in all ecclesiastical matters and administration, and, indeed, to elevate the patriarch to the point that his authority would overshadow that of the tsar in all church matters.[36]

Nikon failed in his endeavor, but the memory of his efforts lingered long afterwards. To the secular authority, the patriarchate remained a potential source of competition and even of danger. Half a century after Nikon's deposition from the patriarchate, reaction to his venture was felt in the *Spiritual Regulation*. Referring to the reasons for the establishment of the Spiritual College, it contains the observation that

> . . . the fatherland need have no fear of revolts and disturbances from a conciliar administration such as proceed from a single, independent ecclesiastical administrator. For the common people do not understand how the spiritual authority is distinguishable from the autocratic; but marveling at the dignity and glory of the Highest Pastor, they imagine that such an administrator is a second Sovereign, a power equal to that of the Autocrat, or even greater than he, and that the pastoral office is another, and a better, sovereign authority.[37]

Differing in its emphasis from Nikon's formulations, the resolution of the council of 1667 approximated the Byzantine ideal, expressed in the *Epanagoge,* of "symphony" and "parallelism" in the functions of the state and church.[38] Consonant with this ideal, the council was able to lay the groundwork for the abolition in 1677 of the Central Administration of Monasteries (restored with a revised function under Peter) and the withdrawal of lay functionaries assigned to the bishops by the state. To this extent the council succeeded in investing the ecclesiastical administration with a measure of independence. However, the council's actions were to have unforeseen repercussions on the future of the Russian church. By their insistence on distinguishing between secular and spiritual spheres of authority, the Russian bishops who participated in the council, in contrast to the Greek hierarchs who were present, took the lead in promoting a distinction that contributed to undermining the notion of goals shared in common by tsar and patriarch.[39] It is a historical irony that, in belatedly seeking to assert the church's independence on the basis of ideological patterns stretching into the Byzantine past, the Russian episcopate was partly responsible for the emergence of a wholly new and different kind of state in Russia, one defining its goals in terms of temporal interests and treating the church as another arm of the state apparatus for advancing the common good.

The turbulent period of Nikon's patriarchate saw a profound crisis erupt in Russian religious and cultural life, precipitated by a second aspect of his reforming activity. Tactlessly and harshly, he

strove to bring church ritual and practice in line with models existing at the time in the Greek church. Opposition to the reforms was
voiced by the Old Believers, on the grounds that they were contrary
to the practices of their ancient faith, sanctioned in the preceding
century by a church council of Russian bishops,[40] and would substitute a different religion for the true one. Archpriest Avvakum, a
spokesman for this view of the sanctioned practices, said: "I hold to
this even unto death, as I have received it. . . . It has been laid
down before us: let it lie thus unto the ages of ages." [41]

Commenting on the stand taken by Avvakum, which did indeed,
in the year of Peter's coronation, 1682, lead to his execution by
burning, Dmitri Obolensky points to the Byzantine tradition in Rus'
as the source of opposition by Old Believers to innovation:

> Thus did a Russian parish priest, in his heroic refusal to counte-
> nance the slightest deviation from the sacred wholeness of the li-
> turgical practice, echo the words of the Byzantine Patriarch Photius,
> who wrote eight centuries previously: "Even the smallest neglect of
> the traditions leads to the complete contempt for dogma." [42]

This opposition was denounced as schismatic by the official
church even though no essential doctrinal disputes or differences
were involved. Nevertheless the measures of reform, pursued with
rigor, raised doubts concerning the traditional role of the church as
the repository of the true faith, and issues implying doctrinal differences were readily come by on both sides. This religious turmoil was
but one symptom of an internal contradiction between the old and
new existing in Muscovite culture, a growing contradiction that created deep fissures in the social structure of the Muscovite state. According to Kapterev the effects of Nikon's ecclesiastical reform were
not confined to church life, but had considerably broader significance, and were organically linked with the whole of contemporary
Russian life.[43] He describes the conditions that brought it about:

> . . . it appeared and became possible only because the former foun-
> dations and supports of Russian life had been considerably rotted
> and shaken. . . . it showed the bankruptcy of our old ideal of Rus-
> sian life, formulated by our bookmen on the basis of narrow na-
> tional self-opinion, on an exaggerated conception of the extraordi-
> nary eminence of old Russian piety and on its utter degeneration
> among all other Orthodox peoples, and at the same time, on a su-
> perstitious-timorous relationship to any new direction in life, even

though called forth by the pressing requirements and demands of
life itself.[44]

It is clear that Kapterev's evaluation of old Russian culture justi-
fies the aim of Nikon's reform if not the manner of its undertaking.
He does not specify here, beyond pointing to the influence of the
contemporary Greek clergy, what the "new directions in life" were
under which Muscovite culture was buckling, but he does suggest
that they were to lead to Peter's *Spiritual Regulation*. It is scarcely
conceivable that much progress would have been made along the
lines of any "new directions" unless there had first occurred an event
like Nikon's ecclesiastical reform, for such progress would have been
impeded by "the general prevalence of pre-Nikonian ideals of life"
and "a general faith in their sacredness, inviolability, and obligation
upon each person." [45] Under the impact of Nikon's reform, however,
this homogeneity of Russia's Orthodox Christian culture had already
started to dissipate before Peter became tsar. The reform left behind
a church weakened from below through the loss of substantial support from those people who, with their intense devotion to the Orthodox faith as they knew it from their fathers, could have provided
strong centers for organized resistance to the execution of Peter's
measures.

Peter's immediate predecessor, Fedor III (1676–82), undertook a reform of the system that determined the qualifications of
persons and families for state service. In abolishing the so-called system of precedence,[46] Fedor attributed his action in the ukase of 12
January 1682 to the application of principles that guided the exercise of his tsarist authority, among which was that of the "common
good." Alexander Lappo-Danilevsky detects in that use of the term
the first incipient trace of the same meaning that it was to acquire
in the time of Peter. For although the presence of religious overtones in the phrasing of Fedor's ukase is undeniable, "the religious
idea of the state in Russia underwent a certain evolution, thanks to
which it began to approach the secular idea of the state." [47]

A number of other political, cultural, social, and religious factors,
often subtly intertwined, entered into the secularization of the state
in Muscovite Rus'. Among them, according to Lappo-Danilevsky,
were: the heresy of the Judaisers in the fifteenth and sixteenth centuries, an ostensibly religious movement that grew to entangle cul-

tural and political issues as well; the reverberations of the Renaissance, the Reformation, and the Counter Reformation, transmitted to Muscovite Rus' first through Poland and after 1667 through Kiev; acquaintance with, and the manifest enthusiasm for, Western achievements in technology, culture, and thought on the part of Peter and his contemporaries through personal contacts and through literature, especially the Protestant literature [48] that was made available in Muscovite Rus'.[49]

The cumulative effect of such influences was telling, both on Russian culture and on the Russian church, between which there had been an indivisible bond in the Muscovite period. Russians began to react to new ideas and cultural patterns—sometimes unaware that it was to such influences that they were reacting. In the seventeenth century, an increasing number of Russians began to address themselves to questions raised by those influences in terms dictated by conceptualizations that had also evolved abroad. In doing so, they ceased to seek solutions in accordance with the traditional frames of reference of their native culture, often simply dissociating themselves from the questions and concepts that had once vitally occupied them. These manifestations were symptomatic of the "new directions in life," at the heart of the far-reaching struggle in which the civilization of Muscovite Rus' was to receive "its death blow at the hands of the reforming Tsar." [50]

IV

Except for one brief month at the very outset, Peter did not reign alone during the first fourteen years after his accession to the throne in April 1682. Instead, after May of the same year, he shared a curious dual monarchical title ("Great Sovereigns, Tsars, and Grand Princes") [51] with his half brother Ivan V. This unparalleled dignity had been thrust upon them both as the outcome of a struggle between rival factions at court waged against a backdrop of popular unrest.

Upon their joint accession neither Peter, then ten years of age, nor Ivan, fifteen, was admitted to the precincts of power. Although the dynamic Peter would one day storm his way into those precincts, Ivan was fated to suffer all his life from chronic physical and mental impairment. Sickly and weak, he had no interest in the high station foisted upon him by persons whose political and personal ambitions were played out in an arena of whose existence he remained largely unmindful. In the midst of turbulence, he clung ever more steadfastly to a life of ascetic religious practices. Notwithstanding the efforts by Peter's opponents to manipulate Ivan for their own ends and to assert his greater rights to the throne as a pretext for advancing their own fortunes, Peter did not fall into an attitude of hostility toward his shy and withdrawn kinsman, but displayed instead genuine signs of warm attachment. Ivan's marriage in 1684 appeared to have a beneficial effect on his general state of health, but politically he remained to the end of his life a neutral, pliable figure who, while court intrigues eddied about him, never took more than a passing interest or passive part in them.

On 29 January 1696, at the age of twenty-nine, Ivan V died. Within a year afterward, with Peter as sole tsar, the process of church secularization through legislation by the state began to accelerate with a rapidity and purposefulness for which there had been no precedent in the Muscovite period. Yet, Ivan's passing had nothing to do with unleashing this movement, just as his presence during life had nothing to do with holding it back. It was merely coincidental that the year of his death corresponded to a turning point in the history of the relations between church and state in Russia. But it was far from coincidental that also in 1696, just shortly after Ivan's death, Peter left Moscow for Voronezh, seat of preparations for his second campaign against the fortified Turkish city of Azov, the first having failed ignominiously the year before.[52]

These two Azov campaigns constituted Peter's first serious military efforts against a real adversary. Through them he was creating a reputation in Europe and learning valuable lessons in tactics, training, and logistics. But tuition in the school of war was high: the required payments pressed heavily upon a population already straining under monetary and manpower exactions leveled upon it by a government whose military expenditures as early as 1680, even before Peter's reign, were already consuming half of the total annual revenues of the state.[53] Under Peter that percentage was to grow even higher, during one especially trying year (1705) by as much as an additional 46 percent. It finally declined to the still sizable total of 63 percent in 1724, the last full year of Peter's reign (and the first year of peace in over three and a half decades!).[54]

It is this context that provides the clue to the motive for Peter's early ecclesiastical legislation and the direction that it took. Within this context can be understood the rationale for Peter's ukases of this time and their tenor, emphasizing at first as they did the preservation of the church's economic resources and later on their exploitation.

The series of measures began with a charter that Peter's administration dispatched in December 1696 to church authorities for compliance.[55] It prohibited metropolitans, archbishops, bishops, archimandrites, and hegumens from making unscheduled expenditures from their treasuries without a ukase from the tsar; it initiated state control over certain of their financial accounting procedures; and it made monasterial and ecclesiastical construction projects contingent upon prior state approval.

The following years saw similar ukases issued. One promulgated in 1698 decreed the cessation of the sovereign's *ruga* (the tsar's prestimony, i.e., allowance in money or kind) to certain Siberian churches enjoying the possession of lands and other profitable holdings.[56] Significant was the reason given in the ukase for its promulgation: it was admitted that, because of the impoverishment of the state treasury, deficiencies had been allowed to occur in the payment of salaries in money and grain to the serving people (*sluzhilye liudi*), who, constituting the backbone of the army, were sorely needed for defense against the enemy.

The purpose of this legislation was quite frankly stated. The adequacy of state revenues, principally for the expenses of military operations, had to be insured. The matter was one of husbanding the state's resources for war. In this case the war happened to be against the Ottoman Empire, but far more exhausting and expensive conflicts with more formidable enemies lay in the offing. Only much later could a coherent and systematic approach to legislation be undertaken, removed from the exigent demands of an unpredictable military involvement. Meanwhile, with all their disjointedness and transitoriness, it is still with justification that, for the church, these early ukases can be viewed as portents of the future, as "the first bell-tone of forthcoming reforms."[57]

After the death in 1700 of Adrian, patriarch of Moscow and primate of the Russian Orthodox church,[58] the tsar abstained from authorizing the formal procedure of nomination and selection of a new patriarch to end the disruption in the church's hierarchical organiza-

tion caused by the vacancy. For twenty years Peter in effect refused
to allow the naming of a successor to the patriarchal throne. Instead, in December 1700, he appointed as *locum tenens* Stefan Iavorsky, metropolitan of Riazan' and Murom, formerly the hegumen
of a monastery [59] and close assistant to the metropolitan of Kiev.[60]
During the years before his death in 1722, Iavorsky's authority and
influence in the post that he grew desperately to dislike diminished
to figurehead dimensions. In those two decades, secular authority
was increased in matters of ecclesiastical administration and discipline, nullifying what gains had been won by the clergy in their
claim to independence in 1667. The patriarchal judicature was abolished, and matters that had been subject to patriarchal authority, except those pertaining to dogma and canon law, were given over to
various secular central administrative offices.[61] The Central Administration of Monasteries was restored and received control of church
revenues,[62] signaling an end to the economic independence of the
church.[63] Finally, the capacity for self-determined action by the
church hierarchy was increasingly restricted.[64] In all these cases legislation generated by the state gave direction to the process of
church secularization; conversely, a sign of increasing secularization
was the very growth of such legislation.

Out of that legislation a number of enactments were repeated, revised, or amplified in the *Spiritual Regulation* [65] and especially in
the subsequent Supplement to the *Spiritual Regulation,* which can
be considered an integral part of the *Regulation* itself.[66] Consequently the *Regulation,* with its Supplement, possesses some features
of a codification. It is, however, more than that, for the tendency toward secularization was reinforced and complemented: the very
claim to autonomy in the internal functioning of the church was in-
validated; and the need for appointing a successor to the patriarchal
throne was obviated. Regarding it as his right, even his duty, and
without explicitly abolishing the patriarchate, the tsar established
the Spiritual College, designating it as the highest ecclesiastical office of the Russian church and naming himself the supreme judge
over it. Thus the ecclesiastical administration was not only subordi-
nated to the secular authority, it was incorporated into the organization of state administrative institutions, in which capacity it was expected "to govern all spiritual activities within the All-Russian
Church" [67] and "to further everything that may bear on faithful ser-

vice and benefit to His Tsarist Majesty." [68] In ministering to spiritual needs, the state itself determined not only their nature, but also the manner in which they should be cared for.[69] In rendering service to the tsar, even ecclesiastical forms and objectives were treated in a new light: their utility in promoting the interests of the state. This deprived even sacraments of their purely religious significance, at least in the external aspects of their administration by the priests.[70]

In important respects the implementation of the program for ecclesiastical reform outlined in the *Spiritual Regulation* did not accord with the intentions of its originators. In the first place, not all the objectives of the *Spiritual Regulation* were realized. This was most evident in the fate of the Spiritual College, which was founded in accordance with the provisions of the manifesto of 25 January 1721 (see pp. 3–4 for its translation). It met but once. Then the name "Spiritual College" disappeared and the assemblage became known instead as the "Most Holy Ruling Synod," [71] a transformation that carried implications transcending mere terminological change.[72] (Speculation arose later among historians as to whose influence prompted the change and why.[73] When prospects of redefining the legal status of the church appeared auspicious in the years before 1917, opinions also were put forward on the seemingly questionable canonical foundations on which the Synod had been established.[74]) In the second place, Peter's ecclesiastical measures failed to gain wholehearted acceptance in the church.[75] They retained their complexion as a form of external coercion, in consequence of which the Petrine reform, in Florovsky's words, "forced the church body to shrink, but did not find a sympathetic echo in the depths of church consciousness." [76]

In addition to the *Spiritual Regulation* and its Supplement, other pronouncements having the force of law were issued at about the same time. Together they make up the corpus of Petrine ecclesiastical legislation that defined the legal status of the Russian church as an institution included in the body politic and subject to the secular authority: in short, an established church. These additional enactments have been grouped under six entries in the sixth volume of the *Complete Collection of the Laws of the Russian Empire* and fall in three categories: tsarist resolutions, usually referred to in English as "imperial resolutions" for the period after 1721; [77] a declaration from the Most Holy Ruling Synod; [78] and an instruction to the emperor's lay representative in the Synod, the oberprocurator.[79] Some of these pronouncements explicated or partly modified certain provisions of the *Spiritual Regulation;* others altered the letter and spirit of it, though they did not change the newly formulated subordinate position of the church vis-à-vis the state. By successfully establishing in law the principle of the ecclesiastical administrative subordination to the authority of the "All-Russian Autocrat," [80] the *Spiritual Regulation* marked the furthest advance yet in the process of church secularization in Russia.

V

Peter's ecclesiastical measures were not an accidental by-product in the successive stages of the Petrine reforms.[81] Rather they were an integral and important part of the sizable body of legislation that initiated and directed the transformation of the Muscovite state in the first quarter of the eighteenth century, from which it emerged as the Russian Empire.

A total of more than three thousand ukases, statutes, charters, treaties, manifestoes, regulations, and other enactments were initiated in Peter's reign. He wrote a great number of them himself and personally supervised the composition of many others.[82] They appeared with increasing frequency in the course of Peter's reign, growing into a formidable body of legislation that touched Russian life—customs, practices, conventions—at many points and affected the church as well as secular institutions. Since in the ecclesiastical and secular spheres this legislation originated in the temporal ruler, it is not surprising to find parallel developments occurring at about the same time in both spheres. The forward course of Petrine ecclesiastical legislation leading to the enactment of the *Spiritual Regulation,* is thus a part of the entire reform movement.

The legislation impelling that movement underwent both qualitative and quantitative changes over a period of some twenty-five years. About five hundred enactments from 1700 to 1709 have been included in the *Complete Collection of the Laws of the Russian Empire* (which, while it is in fact far from being a complete collection, as its title asserts, does nevertheless provide a relative measure of legislative activity). From 1709 to the end of 1719, there were 1,238 enactments entered. Then, in the single five-year period from 1720 to the first part of 1725, before Peter's death on 28 January 1725, almost as many are recorded as in the preceding decade.[83]

This acceleration of legislative activity coincided with the advantage gained by Russian arms in the hard-fought conflict with Sweden, the Northern War (1700–1721). In 1709, after an initial series of disasters and a thorough reorganization of his military forces, Peter won a decisive campaign, culminating with the battle of Poltava, against the Swedish king, Charles XII. Victory exacted a heavy price, however. Aside from the high toll in human suffering and the unstinted expenditure of resources, it was accompanied by "the ruin of the old state order." [84] Subsequently some attempts were made to remedy the deficiencies in the central administration by means of constructive, viable solutions, but it was not until after about 1717 that Peter could address himself to the task of reorganization.

The design for that reorganization was, in part, a secondary consequence of the war itself, for Peter's opponents were the very persons whose technical knowledge and ability to set up "sound procedures" [85] he greatly admired and hastened to adopt in Russia. In the vivid insight offered by Paul Miliukov,

> These "sound procedures" appear to Peter as some kind of secret —like a new tactical maneuver or a rifle of improved type— which foreigners keep to themselves and which need only be discovered for everything to run smoothly.[86]

To discover the key that would open for him, as it had for others, the "sound procedures," Peter sent an agent to Sweden, with instructions to copy clandestinely the statutes and regulations that he found there.[87] After having had them translated and introduced in Russia, Peter expected to see them become effective in producing the changes he desired.[88]

If this approach betrayed a certain naïve view of man and society, and was discredited by the failure of many Petrine reforms, it was quite in keeping with the scientific and humanistic thought of Western Europe at the time, an approach that led to faith in progress and in the efficacy of well-organized institutions for promoting progress. From the West, Peter received advice that a state can be led to a flourishing condition only by means of good institutions,[89] and in his desire to establish such institutions, projects for reforms were

submitted by persons outside Russia. Among them were the German
philosopher-mathematician, Gottfried von Leibnitz,[90] and the English philanthropist-orientalist, Francis Lee.[91] Like others of wide-ranging interests schooled in the West, they were inspired by a desire to see propagated the knowledge and the institutions of the
West, which they hoped would be adopted for the benefit of those in
whose countries they had failed to materialize. These well-intentioned savants, however, neglected to consider that their efforts
might be harmfully disruptive of indigenous ideas and cultural patterns whose evolution had made them inconsistent with the rapid
assimilation of Western knowledge and the formation of Western
institutions.

Juxtaposed to the desire by foreigners to teach was Peter's desire
to learn from them and apply what he learned. Nor was his penchant for seeking Western knowledge and methods limited to technical or organizational information; it included theoretical constructs as well. Indeed, Peter's concept of the sovereign authority of
the Russian monarch was expressed in borrowed terms. According to
that formulation the Russian monarch was one

> who owes no answer to anyone in this world concerning his actions, but has the force and power to rule all his States and lands
> according to his will and gracious consideration as a Christian sovereign.[92]

That definition, as Marc Szeftel notes, based on the text of the Riksdag's decision of 1693, was translated literally from Swedish into
Russian.[93]

As Peter's legislative activity increased, the measures tended to
become more complex: a single ukase would embrace a whole series
of the most diverse subjects.[94] They were issued by a growing number of central administrative institutions. Earlier in Peter's reign, his
personal ukases were the most common form of legislative enactment, and were usually confined to a single topic. A longer ukase
might treat a particular matter in several of its aspects; yet most of
the early ukases were no more than notes that called for additional
enactments to complete them or were statements of general principles that required further elaboration. In many instances they were
incomplete, redundant, contradictory, or simply poorly thought out,
as Peter frankly admitted when he set about to rescind or amend

them, or to postpone their implementation. As a whole, they were efforts to meet the exigencies of the moment, most of which arose as urgent military and financial demands connected with waging the Northern War.[95] Only after his military fortunes improved was Peter able to approach the enactment of measures more or less systematically, to consolidate his legislation, and to devote more time to the solution of administrative problems apart from the endeavor "to extract from the population the greatest strength and the most resources." [96]

War existed as a condition of daily life throughout almost all of Peter's reign.[97] It was within the context of the Northern War in particular that Peter visualized his own legislative activity as it pertained not only to secular institutions but to the church as well. In 1722, making reference to a history of the Northern War that he contemplated be written, he bade:

> Enter in the history that which was accomplished in this war: the measures, civil and military; the regulations of both sorts and ecclesiastical.[98]

Implicit in this statement is the first of the two striking characteristics of Petrine legislation observed by Michael Bogoslovsky: its sweeping range.[99] In this it differed from legislation of the Muscovite period, which consisted largely of procedural law, defining means of redressing infringements of substantive rights. Petrine legislation, on the other hand, appeared "as being all-embracing, touching all aspects of the subject's life": [100] registration at birth, dress and physical appearance, social deportment, spiritual well-being during life, and manner of interment after death. Whatever affected the common good of the state was its proper concern and was subject to regulation—and the religious life of the people was no exception. Of course the tsars of Muscovite Rus', as mentioned earlier,[101] also had taken an active interest in religious issues and frequently exerted a decisive influence in this field.[102] When they did so, however, they acted as protectors of the Orthodox faith.[103] Accordingly, their actions reflected teachings already admitted in the church and were directed toward bringing about conformity with standards of belief and practice held by the church to be true and valid. The secular and spiritual powers in Muscovite Rus' possessed not only an identity of goals but also common recognition of the means, through membership in the mystical life of the church, by which those goals were to be attained. "For the Christian basileus the *summum bonum* was determined by the church." [104] When religious practices appeared to deviate from standards that were thought to be ancient and, hence, correct, the tsar supported the efforts of the patriarch in introducing acceptable forms and suppressing those considered erroneous or corrupt. In Petrine legislation, although the Russian monarch continued to be called "guardian of the true faith and of all good order in the Holy Church," [105] yet the *summum bonum* was no longer determined by the church but by the absolute secular authority.[106] A noticeable change of attitude, inclining toward indifference, took place with regard to formerly vital questions of doctrine, and they were relegated to the judicial competence of the church as formulator and guardian of canon law. Even so, the state did not shirk from prescribing how church doctrine was to be studied.[107] Moreover, as caretaker of the common weal, the state passed on the validity of norms governing the conduct of religious practices, with the express purpose of extirpating superstition and ignorance,[108] arrogating to itself functions formerly carried out by the church.

In so doing, it became more than merely the guardian of the church. Quite apart from reliance on church tradition, the state assumed the responsibility for public welfare in both its material and spiritual aspects, meaning the satisfaction also of the religious requirements of the people. Still, the state did not presume to fulfill this responsibility wholly with its own secular bureaucracy, and accordingly the clergy were once more brought back into the picture. It was the state that now delegated to the clergy their responsibility and invested them with their authority to carry on the ministry, a responsibility that previously rested on the church, supported by the state. Henceforth, only within the limits of the delegation of responsibility and conferral of authority by the state was the church granted a place in law and in the social and political structure of the country. And that position was made conditional upon the church's ability to function in accordance with the state-determined criterion of its usefulness to the state.[109]

In keeping with that criterion, obligations other than that of caring for the spiritual condition of the subjects were imposed on the clergy, absorbing them into the growing bureaucracy of the state for the performance of administrative functions. Both the nature and the number of these functions differed from the judicial-administrative tasks performed earlier by hierarchs as holders of large landed estates. It was sought to make all the clergy, with whatever wealth, prestige, skills, and powers they possessed, available to the state for such diverse tasks as reporting information of political import gathered during confession; [110] promulgating ukases and instructions from the pulpit; [111] collecting levies from parish households and other sources of church revenues; [112] maintaining a growing number of statistical records and forwarding data based on them to state agencies (with the compulsory use of specially marked paper, bearing the state seal); [113] educating, or abetting in the education of, the young in schools and adults in churches according to programs of instruction and sources for sermons prescribed by the state; [114] harboring in monasteries persons retired from military service; [115] incarcerating, likewise in monasteries, under conditions of hard labor, old and feeble persons condemned for criminal offenses; [116] establishing public hospitals, or lazarettos, in monasteries; [117] and punishing crimes against tsar and state by spiritual anathematization.[118] Thus the church as an arm of the state was intended, together with other state institutions, to help insure the strength and safety of the state and promote the common good.

What constituted the common good, it was felt, could be determined by a method [119] cultivated in the intellectual evolution of Western Europe, where the exaltation of reason furnished the appellative for an age. "Reason suggesteth convenient Articles of Peace, upon which men may be drawn to agreement," said a spokesman of that period.[120] Reliance on the application of reason did away with the need for reliance on custom. Custom, though challenged and shaken in the second half of the seventeenth century, still dominated almost every aspect of Muscovite culture, and accordingly the most minute details of social and private life were not immune from scrutiny and change through legislation thought to be based on the light of reason.[121]

Steeped thus in the philosophy of natural law, which stressed the universality of reason and of the presence of the reasoning process in all men, Petrine legislation exhibited a second characteristic noted by Bogoslovsky: its appeal to reason.[122] To be sure the warnings common to Muscovite legislation were not abandoned, and potential offenders were given either explicit descriptions of, or indefinite allusions to, the punishments that would befall them in consequence of their crimes. Entire articles taken from the earlier legislation were sometimes included; yet there was present also an unfamiliar element: explanatory clauses calculated to induce obedience by influencing the reason. Words and phrases such as "wherefore" and "for the reason that" became prominent fixtures in Petrine legislation. Nor were they mere embellishments. It was intended that the enactments do more than simply prescribe or proscribe; they must persuade as well. And that could be done only by the presentation of what was deemed to be convincing proof that could be apprehended and acceded to by the mind of rational man. Consequently individual enactments often acquired the tenor of polemic or didactic tracts. The *Spiritual Regulation* originated as such a tract, which, when it became law, retained much of its former quality, characterized by the support through argumentation imparted to its prescriptive articles.

The content, form, and scope of Petrine legislation—its broad range of interests; its adoption of a new conceptual system from abroad; its eclectic and superficial combining of past norms; the vigor of its phraseology; its concern for the common good, combined with an often ruthless severity in prescribing punishments; its vision of the church as a means for state action—mirrored the mental disposition and personality of its chief legislator, Peter himself.

In his personal life Peter maintained an unexpectedly large number of habits or fancies out of the Muscovite past,[123] but it is doubtful that he understood their significance. Says Vasilii Kliuchevsky: "To the end, he was unable to understand either the historical logic or the physiology of national life." [124] Contributing, perhaps, to Peter's lack of desire to understand was his ugly encounter as a child with persons representative of the old culture. At the age of ten he was immersed in a terrifying drama of rebellion and sanguinary conflict for the throne.[125] With his life and the lives of his family at stake, he saw how the clergy kept silent, carrying out the will of the rebels.[126] It was as if "Old Rus' stood up then and was exposed before Peter in all its work and fruits." [127] After that episode, Peter's estrangement from Muscovite life began, first in the Western military atmosphere of Preobrazhenskoe and under the informal tutelage of the inhabitants of the German suburb outside Moscow; [128] later through the counsels and instructions of kings, philosophers, and

carpenters in Europe.[129] Not unimportant in Peter's development
was the custom, widespread in Muscovite Rus' and prior to Peter's
reign at least tacitly condoned by the church, of marriages arranged
for young couples by their families without the consent of the former.[130] Peter was a partner in such a marriage at sixteen, which
as the outcome of "a matter of intrigue" [131] brought together two
incompatible persons in an unhappy union.[132] The results, Verkhovskoi suggests, fostered in Peter an indifference to the moral virtues
preached by the church and further alienated him from the values of
the past.[133] It becomes less of a paradox, then, that at the instigation of the tsar the power of the state was pitted against the cultural
values of the past or that the purpose of the state, as it proceeded in
the struggle, was expressed in legislation reflecting a world view
sharply at variance with those values.

VI

With the growing acceptance of Western categories of thought in
Russia, legislation began to change in terminology and concept. The
transformation meant that it could then be used by the state as an
instrument to bring the emerging Russian Empire closer to the ideal
of an absolute monarchy "of the same kind that had arisen in western Europe during the first centuries of the modern period." [134]

The political doctrine of the absolute authority of the monarch as
expounded by theoreticians in Western Europe found in the Ukrain-
ian reaches of the Muscovite state a receptive mind and articulate
advocate in Feofan Prokopovich.[135]

Peter's first meeting with him in 1706 was unremarkable. Three
years later, however, Prokopovich delivered before the tsar an im-
pressive panegyric commemorating the recent Russian victory over
the Swedes at Poltava. This proved to be the occasion for Prokopovich's admission into the operations of Peter's calculus for turning to
practical account all available trustworthy talent. Later contacts between the two men reinforced Peter's earlier favorable impression of
Prokopovich. The most important consequence of their relationship
occurred in 1718 when Peter entrusted to Prokopovich the composition of the *Spiritual Regulation*.[136]

Prokopovich's natural endowments and high caliber of formal
training had equipped him well for this assignment. Born in Kiev in

1681, he began his higher studies at the Kiev Academy, where teaching followed the pattern of Roman Catholic, and particularly Jesuit, colleges and academies.[137] Later he journeyed to study in Lwów, Kraków, Florence, Pisa, and Rome itself, access to whose classical and scholastic riches he gained by means of a temporary conversion to Catholicism, an expedient not uncommon among young scholars living near the Polish-Lithuanian border who wished to acquire more education than was obtainable in Orthodox countries. In 1704, two years after his return to Kiev and reconversion to Orthodoxy, Prokopovich was admitted to the faculty of the Kiev Academy, where he became a teacher of distinction (advancing progressively from poetics, through rhetoric and philosophy, to theology) and later an able administrator.

The range of his intellectual interests and literary tastes is indicated by the personal library he left after his death in 1736. Amassed over a period of years, its three thousand-odd volumes provided him with a scholarly instrument imposing in its breadth of coverage, whose different resonances Prokopovich skillfully orchestrated in his learned and publicistic writings.[138]

The early rejection by Prokopovich—apparently while still studying in Rome—of traditional Roman Catholic scholasticism, to which most of his counterparts at the Kiev Academy adhered, has never been satisfactorily explained; but in the wake of that rejection, for whatever reason it occurred, he became an outspoken critic of "Latinism." In this he concurred with the acerbic opinion of his correspondent, the German Lutheran theologian and scholar, Johann Franz Buddeus (Budde): "The Catholic Church raises to the level of dogma ignorance, barbarism, and superstition, that is, precisely those characteristics which the Russian tsar by all possible means is trying to eradicate in his people." [139]

Prokopovich's rejection of Roman Catholic scholasticism constitutes a critical element in the development of his personal convictions, which came to correspond to the tenets of Reformation theology, philosophy, and ecclesiology as they emerged in the territories that made up Protestant Germany. What made Prokopovich's convictions important for the Russian church, as well as for Muscovite culture and society with its markedly religious ethos, was that they seemed to express, with few variations, the views held by Peter. Verkhovskoi, in analyzing Prokopovich's political views as expressed in the *Justice of the Monarch's Will*,[140] finds in them three basic propositions:

1. that the secular state authority possesses sovereignty (majesty), wherefore any other authority, and of course the ecclesiastical [authority], does not possess sovereignty, and therefore submits in law to the state authority;
2. the supreme state authority obeys only God and not any human norms, and in that respect it does not obey church canons;
3. by not obeying God, and thus falling into sin, the supreme authority is its own judge in the question whether it has committed sin or not.[141]

On the basis of the community of views shared by Prokopovich and Peter,[142] and of their complementary interaction with each other, in which one expressed those views, the other legislated them, was delineated and fixed in law the future institutional position of the Russian church within the state. That position was thought to be corrective of the defects, conceived of in terms that were anti-Roman Catholic, anti-Greek Empire, and antisuperstitious ignorance (meaning anti-Orthodox), which Peter and Prokopovich ascribed to the Muscovite past and present, projected against the German Protestant ideal of a regulated police state.[143]

A variety of theoretical formulations of this ideal were made by political thinkers in Western Europe, who proposed to deal with the nature, scope, and function of political power as it underwent readjustment following the Protestant Reformation. Pertinent to this discussion is the political concept of the territorial system,[144] the proponents of which viewed the church and state as corporations, or colleges. As such, these colleges were not considered equal. Since, in the Protestant view, every member of the church is equal with every other member in being a Christian, the church lacks the balance or contraposition that exists in the state between ruler and subjects. The church, then, is a college within the state. That the church, during the predominance of the police state,[145] became dependent on the latter was a development completely consistent with the tenets of the territorial system, according to which it is the sovereign in whom reside the rights of the state with regard to the church. His authority over the church is an essential constituent of his supremacy and state authority, although in regard to the church that authority theoretically extends to external matters only, that is, he possesses *jus circa sacra,* while *jus in sacra* continues to remain with the church as a particular corporation within the state. In practice, however, this theoretical distinction tended to become blurred. For, as Verkhovskoi succinctly remarks:

> . . . in view of the difficulty of differentiating between *jura circa sacra* and *jura in sacra,* and also because the right of differentiating between them was passed to the state as a higher form of social interaction, it is obvious that the independence of ecclesiastical authority in practice must be only apparent and must have meaning only by virtue of the discretion of the state and in keeping with the limits set by it.[146]

The thesis of the territorial school, *cujus regio, ejus religio,*[147] was expounded by a group of writers, among whom were Hugo Grotius, Thomas Hobbes, Samuel Pufendorf, Christian Thomasius, Justus Henning Böhmer, and Johann Jakob Moser.[148]

Georges Bissonnette assigns a place of preeminence to the German jurist Pufendorf as the one exponent of the territorial system who had the most influence, directly through his writings and indirectly through Prokopovich, on Peter's vision of the state and the role of the monarch with relation to the church.[149] He sees in Pufendorf the particular focal point of "the spirit of *raison d'état* or 'monarchical rationalism' " in light of which the inner consistency of Petrine ecclesiastical legislation as corresponding to a body of political principles can be understood.[150] It is significant that Peter's personal instruction on the education of his son, Alexis, specified the inclusion of a work by Pufendorf.[151] Among the persons singled out as teachers worthy of study in the *Spiritual Regulation,* the only contemporary so named was Pufendorf.[152] Still, one must not overlook the observation made by Preserved Smith that Pufendorf was not wholly an original thinker, that he "enjoyed wide vogue as combining into a consistent whole the variegated theories of earlier thinkers, particularly those of Grotius and Hobbes." [153] To some extent, then, Pufendorf himself may be seen as a kind of intermediary, in whose writings the sometimes contradictory formulations of political theoreticians in Western Europe assumed a coherent pattern.

Legislation based on the theoretical concepts of the territorial system was contained in ecclesiastical regulations, *Kirchenordnungen,* issued in individual German territories, beginning in 1528, by princes or city magistrates for the regulation of Protestant ecclesiastical organization and worship.[154] In those enactments may be seen prototypes of the *Spiritual Regulation.* Examination shows a great deal of similarity, even in details, between the *Spiritual Regulation* and the "regulations" or "ecclesiastical statutes" for newly established local "general consistories" [155]—in territories accepting the Reformation, princely organs of central control over religious matters received the name "consistories." [156] From that name, an insight into the character of the Spiritual College is provided in a passage from a personal letter written to a friend on 10 May 1720 by Feofan Prokopovich, who, in describing the institution envisioned in the *Spiritual Regulation,* quite frankly calls it, *"Collegium seu Consistorium Ecclesiasticum Generalis."* [157]

For Peter and Prokopovich, a practical example for the design of a consistory was provided by the ecclesiastical reform of King Charles XI of Sweden (1655–97).[158] On 3 September 1686 a new *Kirchenordnung* was enacted, followed on 11 February 1687 by a consistorial statute. On the basis of those laws, the *Consistorium Regni,* which, consisting of deputies of the clergy in council, had formed the highest ecclesiastical body as the final instance of revision and appeal, lost its former significance. Instead, the king assumed authority and direction over all ecclesiastical administration. He obtained the right to appoint bishops and, through them, pastors and other church functionaries, who were obliged to render an oath of loyalty and obedience to him. While the king could intervene in purely ecclesiastical matters, he did not assume the position of *summus episcopus.* He acted rather in the capacity, suggestive of the role ascribed later to the Russian monarch in the *Spiritual Regulation,*[159] of *oberster Schirmherr des christlichen glaubens in seinem Reiche.* Further, Verkhovskoi's analysis of the Swedish documents and his comparison of the *Spiritual Regulation* with them have shown that the *Regulation* is not only similar to, but identical with, those documents in many respects.[160]

The Swedish ecclesiastical reform was not the only example before Peter and Prokopovich. Others, such as in England, where Peter was an enthusiastic and observant visitor, also influenced the future emperor in forming his judgment of a desirable relationship between church and state in Russia.[161]

VII

In writing about Peter's ecclesiastical reforms Bissonnette observes that they possessed a certain inner consistency, and attributes that quality principally to the influence of a single person. Schmemann, in larger perspective, points to the world view within which were formulated Peter's thoughts in regard to the relationship between church and state, and within which the inner consistency evident in his legislation acquires added significance.[162] In this light, Peter's efforts may be seen as having been directed toward importing into the Muscovite state the basic tenets of the Protestant territorial system, in keeping with which the visible church on earth was envisaged as "a religious projection of the state itself." [163] As for the indigenous Orthodox church, it is perhaps not far from the mark to say, as Iurii Samarin did, that Peter simply did not see it.[164] Accordingly it becomes clear why Florovsky calls the *Spiritual Regulation* "a program for a Russian Reformation." [165]

The formation of an established church in Russia may thus be viewed in broad compass as part of a general movement occurring at about the same time in other parts of Europe. Indeed, this development in Russia cannot be fully understood in isolation from that movement. Nevertheless the relationship that came into being between church and state in Russia did not exactly duplicate other attempted solutions of this problem in other countries. As the Russian emperor's *Spiritual Regulation* was not the Swedish king's *Kirchenordnung,* neither was it the English king's *Act of Supremacy,* though they shared, in varying degrees, a common inspiration, a common purpose, and a common idiom (different languages notwithstanding). In Russia a historically dominant secular authority had presided over an ecclesiastical hierarchy whose position in regard to the state ordinarily was one of dependence. However, there had been a unity of goals shared by church and state, based on Orthodox Christian tradition, which while it lasted seemed to justify the intervention of the tsars in ecclesiastical matters. With Peter that conceptual unity disapppeared and the state espoused a new mission. It discarded the norms and ignored the categories of thought that had been upheld by the church and that had, conversely, themselves supported the institutional autonomy of the church in law. One further step would bring the process to a logical conclusion. That step was taken when, through the enactment of the *Spiritual Regulation,* the state institutionalized, within a secular frame of reference, the subordination of the church.

NOTE ON THE TRANSLATION

The system of transliterating the Cyrillic alphabet in this translation, as well as in the preceding introduction, is that employed in the transliteration of Russian by the Library of Congress. It has been modified in two respects: (1) all ligatures and other diacritical marks have been omitted; and (2) except for titles in the bibliography, the suffix that would ordinarily be rendered as "skii" is instead given as *sky:* thus "Iavorskii" becomes *Iavorsky;* "monastyrskii," *monastyrsky,* etc. Words that have commonly accepted English equivalents are used in place of transliterated Russian forms: e.g., *Peter, Alexis,* and *hegumen* instead of "Petr," "Alexiei," and "igumen," respectively.

Biblical passages in the translation are taken from the *New Catholic Edition of the Holy Bible.* In addition, however, the *Holy Bible: Revised Standard Version* has also been used, in lieu of the former, where it appeared to correspond more closely to the precise shade of meaning conveyed by a Biblical or exegetical passage in the *Spiritual Regulation.* In such cases the abbreviation "RSV" appears after the citation in the notes.

Regulation of the Spiritual College

including

the Manifesto of 25 January 1721, the Oath
of the Members of the Spiritual College, and
the Supplement to the Spiritual Regulation

The Manifesto of 25 January 1721

AMONG the many cares derived from the obligation of our God-given authority concerning the reform of our nation and of other states subject to us, we have given consideration also to the clergy.[1] Perceiving in it much disorder and great deficiency in its affairs, we have experienced in our conscience a not unfounded fear that we appear ungrateful to the All-High if, having received from Him so much good success in reforming not only the military class but likewise the civil service, we should neglect the reform also of the ecclesiastical estate. And when He, the impartial Judge, asks from us a reckoning concerning this great commission entrusted to us by Him, let us not be without reply. Wherefore, following the example of former pious kings who, as in the Old, so in the New Testament,[2] undertook to care for the reform of the clergy and envisaged no better means for that than a conciliar administration (for no single person exists without weakness, and moreover, if authority is not hereditary, it is for that reason safeguarded even less),[3] we do establish the Spiritual College, that is, a spiritual conciliar administration, which, in accordance with the following *Regulation,* shall govern all spiritual activities within the All-Russian Church. We command all our faithful subjects of every class, spiritual and secular, to hold this as a vital and powerful administration, to seek from it final adjudications, decisions, and settlements of spiritual cases, to be satisfied with its determined judgment, and to obey its ukases in everything, subject to great punishment for resistance and disobedience, as with the other Colleges.

This College must supplement its *Regulation* with new rules in the future, such as different occasions may require for different cases. However, the Spiritual College must not do this without our consent.

We ordain that in the Spiritual College these members be appointed: one president, two vice-presidents, four councilors, four assessors.

Whereas it is mentioned in this *Regulation,* in Part I, Articles 7 and 8, that the president, if he manifestly errs in something, shall be subject to the judgment of his peers, that is, of this College, we therefore ordain that he shall have a single vote, equal with the others.

All members of this College, before entering upon their work, shall take this oath, or promise, on the Holy Gospel, in accordance with the affixed form of the oath.[4]

The Oath of the Members of the Spiritual College

I, NAMED hereunder, promise and swear by Almighty God, on His Holy Gospel, that I am in duty bound, and am resolved to fulfill my duty. I will endeavor by all possible means, in the councils, tribunals, and in all proceedings of this spiritual administrative council, always to seek the very truth and justice, and to act in all things according to the provisions contained in the *Spiritual Regulation* and in keeping with whatever future determinations may be made by the concurrence of this spiritual administration and the consent of His Tsarist Majesty. I will act in all these things according to my conscience—unenslaved by partiality, unafflicted by rancor, envy, or obstinacy and, simply, not captivated by passions, but in the fear of God, always bringing to mind His incorruptible judgment—and with an openhearted love of God and neighbor, regarding as the ultimate purpose of all my thoughts, words, and deeds, the glory of God, the salvation of human souls, and the edification of the whole Church, striving not as if it were mine, but because it is that of Lord Jesus. I swear by the living God that I will always remember His terrible word: Condemned is he who does God's work with negligence. In every dealing of this administrative council I will act as if it were God's work, without sloth and with all possible diligence, to the utmost of my strength, forsaking all my comfort and rest. I will not presume upon my inexperience, but if I encounter doubt in regard to anything, I will in every way endeavor to seek understanding and knowledge from the Holy Scriptures, the conciliar canons, and the accepted beliefs of the great, ancient teachers. Again, I swear by Almighty God that I resolve, and am in duty bound, to be a faithful, good, and obedient slave and subject to my natural and true Tsar and Sovereign, Peter the First, Autocrat of All Russia, etc.; and after him, to Their Highnesses, the legitimate Heirs of His Tsarist Majesty, who, by the pleasure and autocratic authority of His Tsarist Majesty, are selected and will in the future be selected and honored for acceptance of the throne; and to Her Majesty, Our Sovereign, Tsaritsa Ekaterina Aleksieevna. All the rights and prerogatives (or privileges) which have been enacted and will be enacted into law, appertaining to the high sovereignty, power, and authority of His Tsarist Majesty, I will defend and guard to the utmost of my knowledge, strength, and opportunity, and in this I will not spare my life if occasion demands. Moreover, on all occasions, I will try in utmost measure to further everything that may bear on faithful service and benefit to His Tsarist Majesty. As for whatever concerns damage, harm, or loss to His Majesty's interests, as soon as I become aware of it, I will not only inform of it in due time, but will strive by all possible means to avert it and not to tolerate it. Whenever some secret matter, or a matter of any kind, arises that pertains to the service or to the benefit of His Majesty, or of the Church, which I shall be ordered to keep secret, then I will keep it in complete secrecy, and not disclose it to anyone for whom it is not necessary to know about it and to whom it is not directed that it be revealed. I confess with an oath that the final judge of this Spiritual College is the Monarch of All Russia himself, Our Most Gracious Sovereign. Again, I swear by the All-Seeing God that all this now being promised by me is not interpreted differently in my mind from what I have proffered with my lips, but has the very meaning and understanding that the words here written convey to those reading and hearing them. I affirm by my oath, as God Who sees all hearts is Witness of my promise, that it is not false. If it is false and not accordant with my conscience, then may He be a Righteous Avenger to me. In conclusion of this, my oath, I kiss the words and the cross of my Savior. Amen.[5]

The Regulation or Statute of the Spiritual College

BY WHICH IT MAY KNOW ITS OBLIGATIONS,
THOSE OF ALL ECCLESIASTICAL OFFICERS,
AND THOSE OF LAYMEN, INSOFAR AS THEY
ARE SUBJECT TO SPIRITUAL ADMINISTRATION,
AND MOREOVER, BY WHICH IT IS
TO FUNCTION IN THE DISPOSITION
OF ITS AFFAIRS.[6]

THIS *Regulation* is divided into three parts, corresponding [7] to the three spiritual needs deserving of attention and requiring administration, which are:

1. A description of and the important reasons for such an administration.

2. The matters subject to such an administration.

3. The responsibility, function, and power of the administrators themselves.

The basis of government is the Law of God, which has been set forth in the Holy Scriptures, in canons, or the conciliar rules of the holy fathers, and in civil statutes consonant with the word of God. These require special books of their own, and they are not included here.

PART I. WHAT THE SPIRITUAL COLLEGE IS,
AND WHAT THE IMPORTANT REASONS FOR SUCH
AN ADMINISTRATION ARE

An administrative college is nothing more than an administrative assembly in which certain matters are subject to the administration not of a single person but of many who are qualified therefor and are authorized by sovereign authority.

It is not an *ad hoc* college; rather, it is permanent. *Ad hoc* is when qualified individuals meet in regard to one certain matter that has arisen, or in regard to many that require a decision but once. Such are the ecclesiastical synods, and civil tribunals and councils, whenever they undertake an extraordinary investigation.

A permanent college is said to exist when, in certain specific matters, frequently or perennially occurring in the fatherland, a certain sufficient number of qualified men is appointed for their administration.

Such were the ecclesiastical Sanhedrin in the Old Testament Church in Jerusalem, the civil tribunal of the Areopagites in Athens, and other administrative assemblies, called *Dikasteria,* in that same city.

Thus was it also in many other states, as in ancient ones, so in those of the present time.

Such different colleges as correspond to the variety of state matters and needs the Most Sovereign Tsar of All Russia, Peter the First, most wisely established in the year 1718 for the benefit of his dominion, the fatherland.[8]

As a Christian Sovereign, guardian of the true faith and of all good order in the Holy Church, having given consideration to spiritual needs, and desiring every best administration of them, he has vouchsafed to establish also the Spiritual College, which shall diligently and unceasingly look after what is of benefit to the Church, so that everything may proceed in an orderly manner and so that there may not be disorder, for this is the wish of the Apostle and, much more, the benevolent desire of God Himself.

Let no one suppose that this administration is unsuitable and that it would be better for one person to direct the spiritual affairs of the whole commonalty, as some bishops autonomously govern the affairs of separate countries or of eparchies. Here are propounded cogent reasons showing that this permanent conciliar administration, like a perpetual synod or Sanhedrin, is more adequate and better than an administration by a single individual, the more so in a monarchy, such as is our Russian State.

1. In the first place, truth is to be found more certainly by conciliar concurrence than through one individual. There is an ancient Greek proverb: Later thoughts are wiser than first.[9] Moreover, many minds pondering a single issue will be wiser than one. It happens that, in a certain difficulty, a simple person may see what an educated and intelligent person will not see. How, then, is it that there is no need for a conciliar administration, in which many minds analyze a problem that has been presented, and what one does not comprehend, another will understand, and what this one fails to see, the other one will see? Thus, a doubtful matter will be explained more certainly and more quickly, and whatever decision it requires will appear without difficulty.

2. As with certainty of understanding, so also the force of a decision concerning an issue is of importance here, for a conciliar verdict tends toward greater assurance and obedience than the ukase of a single person. The authority of monarchs, whom God Himself commands to obey out of conscience, is autocratic. Nevertheless they have their advisors, not only for the sake of a better quest after truth, but so that willful persons may not be able falsely to allege that a monarch commands this or that more through his own power or whim rather than through judgment or truth. How much more, then, is this so in ecclesiastical administration, where the government is not monarchical and the administrators are commanded that they shall not rule the clergy; [10] where, if a single person enacts something, opponents can, even by slandering once his person, vitiate the force of his enactment, which they would not be able to do where a decree proceeds from conciliar concurrence.

3. This is an especially compelling reason: When an administrative college is under the Sovereign Monarch and has been established by the Monarch, it is evident here that the college is not some faction, constituted through secret association for the sake of its own interests, but individuals assembled for the general welfare by the command of the Autocrat and under his scrutiny, jointly with others.

4. It is also important that, in an administration by a single per-

son, there often occurs a prolongation and interruption of affairs because of unavoidable exigencies arising for the administrator, or because of infirmity and illness. And when he passes away, then matters completely come to a halt. It is different with a conciliar administration: should one member not be in attendance, even if he be the most important person, the others carry on the function, and work progresses in an uninterrupted flow.

5. It is of great benefit that, in such a college, there is not to be found room for partiality, insidiousness, and corrupt judgment. For how is it possible that there could gather together persons in defense of a guilty party, or in condemnation of an innocent party, where, if there is one among them who is partial toward, or inflamed against, the individual being judged, still, some other member, and yet a third member, and the rest are free of that wrath and partiality? How, indeed, can bribery prevail where work is accomplished not through authority, but on the basis of sound and essential principles, and when one is apprehensive of another in that his venality may be revealed (if he does not show an adequate reason for his opinion)? This is especially so when a college consists of such persons that it is quite impossible for any of them to conspire secretly, that is, if they are persons of different ranks and callings: bishops, archimandrites, hegumens, and those in authority from among the white priesthood.[11] In truth, it cannot be conceived here how such as these would dare even to disclose to one another any insidious thoughts, much more that they might agree upon wrongdoing.

6. Likewise a college has in itself the freest spirit for justice. It is not as though a single administrator were to fear the wrath of the powerful, for to search out grounds against many, and especially against persons of different stations, is not so easy as against a single person.

7. This is highly significant: The fatherland need have no fear of revolts and disturbances from a conciliar administration such as proceed from a single, independent ecclesiastical administrator. For the common people do not understand how the spiritual authority is distinguishable from the autocratic; but marveling at the dignity and glory of the Highest Pastor, they imagine that such an administrator is a second Sovereign, a power equal to that of the Autocrat, or even greater than he, and that the pastoral office is another, and a better, sovereign authority. Thus have the people, on their own, become ac-

customed to think. What, then, when the perverse utterances of am-
bitious clerics are added, and they place fire under dry tinder?
Wherefore simple hearts are misdirected by this notion, so that, in
any kind of matter, they do not look so much to the Autocrat as to
the Supreme Pastor. And whenever some discord is perceived between them, they all defer to the ecclesiastical, rather than to the
secular, ruler, however blindly and senselessly, and they venture to
conquer and rebel on his behalf. In doing so the accursed ones flatter
themselves that they conquer in accord with God Himself, and that
they do not defile their hands, but consecrate them, even though
they embark upon the shedding of blood. Those particularly inclined
to such ideas are not the common people, but insidious persons who,
hostile to their Sovereign, when they see a conflict between the Sovereign and the Pastor, snatch at that as a favorable occasion for
their malice, and under the guise of ecclesiastical zeal would not
hesitate to lay their hands upon Christ the Lord. To that iniquity, as
though to the work of God, they stir up the common people. How,
after all, would it be put to rest when even the Pastor himself is in-
flated with such an opinion of himself? It is difficult to say how
great a calamity can arise therefrom.

These are not fancied imaginings, so that it is only possible to
conjecture about this; but in very deed has this appeared more than
once in many states. Do only delve into the history of Constantinople after the period of Justinian, and much of that will appear. And
even the pope was able, by means not different from those, not only
to cut the Roman Empire in half and to appropriate for himself a
great part of it, but more than once even to shake other states almost to final destruction. Let us not recall similar convulsions
among ourselves in the past!

For such evil in a conciliar spiritual administration there is no
room. Since here, even as regards the president himself, there is no
great glory dazzling the people, since there is no excessive splendor
or pageantry, since there is no vainglory surrounding him, flatterers
cannot exalt him with extravagant praise. Whatever good is done
by such an administration is impossible to be attributed to the president alone. The very name "president" is not lofty, for it does not
mean anything more than chairman. Thus, neither he nor anyone
else can think pretentiously of him. And when the people see that
this conciliar administration has been established by the Monarch's

ukase and the Senate's decree, then they will remain all the more meek, and will largely abandon the hope of obtaining help for their rebellions from the clergy.

8. There will accrue also this benefit to the Church and to the state from such a conciliar administration: in it, not only any one of the members, but even the president, or chairman, himself, shall be subject to the judgment of his peers, that is, to that selfsame college, if he manifestly errs in something. This is not done where a single despotic pastor governs, for he would not desire to be judged by bishops subordinate to himself. If he were forced into it, then, nevertheless, among the common people, ignorant of justice and reasoning blindly, such a judgment would be suspect and subject to defamation. From which it follows that, against such an evil tyrant, an ecumenical council would need to be summoned, which can be done only with great difficulty for the whole fatherland, and not without much expense. Indeed, at the present time, it seems absolutely impossible (when the Eastern patriarchs live under the Turkish yoke and the Turks fear our state more than before).

9. Finally, such a conciliar administration will form something like a school of ecclesiastical administration. For, from the communication of many different decisions, and from the counsels and sound arguments that matters frequently arising require, anyone can conveniently learn from his associates about ecclesiastical policy and acquire, through daily habit, the skill by which he might better administer the House of God. Wherefore, those who are the most qualified persons among the colleagues, or associates, will be worthy to ascend to the dignity of the episcopate. And thus, in Russia, with God's help, coarseness will soon fall away from the clergy, and the very best can be hoped for.

PART II.   MATTERS SUBJECT TO THIS ADMINISTRATION

In considering the matters that are to be administered in the Spiritual College, all of them can be classified in two categories.

The first concerns matters of the whole Church generally, applicable to the clergy as well as to the laity, to all degrees of rank, great and small, and to ordinary needy persons, where it is fitting to watch that everything is done properly according to Christian law and where, if something contrary to it is found, one should ask whether there is not a want of such instruction as it is appropriate that every Christian be given, about which a short discussion follows.

The second concerns matters bearing on specific offices. These offices are five in number: (1) bishops, (2) presbyters, deacons, and other church clergy, (3) monks, (4) teachers and students in educational institutions; so also church preachers,[12] (5) laymen, insofar as they are concerned with religious instruction, such as pertains to proper and improper marriages and other matters involving secular persons.

What is important concerning all these offices is here presented seriatim.

Common Matters

Here, in keeping with the aforesaid proposal, it is fitting to consider two matters. First, whether everything is being done properly and according to Christian law and whether anything is being done that is contrary to that law, and where. Second, whether instruction appropriate to Christians is being afforded.

As to the first point, the following articles are applicable.

1. The canticles [13] that have been compiled, and that are being compiled, as well as other church services [14] and public prayers of thanksgiving and petition,[15] of which a great number have been compiled, especially in our time, in Little Russia, shall be examined anew to determine whether those compilations correspond to the true versions and whether they have in them anything contrary to the word of God, or even anything unseemly and senseless.

2. Likewise it shall be determined which of those numerous prayers, although they may be correct, are nevertheless not mandatory for everyone, and may be used privately, according to one's desire, but not in church, lest in time they become law and burden the conscience of man.

3. *The Lives of the Saints* shall be examined to determine whether any of them are falsely fabricated tales, telling what was not, or telling what is contrary to Orthodox Christian teaching, or whether they lack content and are deserving of ridicule. Such tales shall be exposed and prohibited, with a disclosure of the falsity found in them. For such blatantly false tales are contrary to sound teaching. As an example, in the *Life* of Euphrosinus of Pskov,[16] the dispute over the double singing of the *Alleluia* is clearly false, and was

fabricated by some good-for-nothing in whom, besides the worthless dogma of the double *Alleluia,* there are to be found the heresies of Sabellius,[17] Nestorius,[18] and others. Although that writer erred through ignorance, it is nevertheless not fitting for the ecclesiastical administration to allow such fabrications, and instead of healthful spiritual food, to give the people poison. This is especially so when the common people are unable to distinguish between right and left, but tenaciously and stubbornly cling to whatever they see written in a book.

4. It is fitting strictly and diligently to examine those fabrications that lead a person into a bad habit or activity and point the wrong way to salvation. For example, not to work on Friday and to spend it in celebration, saying that *Piatnitsa* [19] grows angry with noncelebrants and sets upon them with great menace; likewise, to fast for twelve designated Fridays for the sake of much physical and spiritual gain; [20] or again, personally to reverence certain church services as being more important when celebrated on particular occasions than at other times: mass on the feast of the Annunciation, matins on Easter, and vespers on Pentecost.[21] These examples are mentioned because they do harm to a few simple people. Care, however, must be exercised on behalf of the few, or on behalf of even a single brother, for whose sake Christ died, lest they be tempted. Nevertheless there are teachings similar to these that are contrived by the most upstanding persons, apparently through their simplicity, and because of that, they are the more harmful. There is a tradition at the Kievan Monastery of the Caves that a person buried there, although he may have died without confession, will be saved.[22] How far these, and tales similar to them, lead away from the path of salvation, everyone, regardless how little versed in Orthodox teaching, provided he is a person of good conscience, must acknowledge, and not without sighing.

5. There can be found certain unnecessary, or even harmful, ceremonies. It is heard that, in Little Russia, in the district of Starodub,[23] on a day set aside as a holyday, they lead a bareheaded girl, whom they name in honor of *Piatnitsa,* in a church procession (if what they say is true), and in front of the church, the people pay respect to her with gifts and in the hope of some benefit. Likewise, in another place, priests pray with the people before an oak; and a

priest distributes the branches of that tree among the people as a blessing. It shall be investigated whether this is indeed being done and whether the bishops of those places know about this. For if these, and other things similar to them, are found, they lead the people into false and shameful idolatry.

6. Wherever any holy relics appear to be doubtful, they shall be examined, for much of this is falsified. For example, certain foreign instances are mentioned: the body of the protomartyr, Saint Stephen, lies both outside Venice, in a Benedictine monastery, in the church of Saint George, and in Rome, in the church of Saint Lawrence-Without-the-Walls; [24] likewise many nails from the cross of the Lord and much milk of the Most Blessed Mother of God are reputedly to be found throughout Italy. Should it not be ascertained whether we also have such frivolity?

7. As regards holy icons, what is written in the vows of bishops being consecrated shall be examined.[25]

8. This also shall be watched, that it not be done in the future as it has been done: It is said that some bishops, to help poor churches, or for new buildings, have commanded that there be searched out the revelation of an icon in the wilderness or at a spring; and on account of the discovery itself, they have testified that this icon is miraculous.

9. A bad and harmful custom, especially repugnant to God, has arisen: to sing church offices and prayer services in two or more parts, so that matins or vespers are broken up into separate portions and are sung at once by several persons. Thus, two or three prayer services are performed simultaneously by several singers and lectors. This has happened and become customary because of the laziness of the clergy. Certainly, such devotions must be abolished.[26]

10. This most exceedingly shameful practice has been discovered: prayers (so it is said) are carried in a hat to people who are far distant by their messengers. This is written as a reminder, so that sometime it might be ascertained whether this is being done.

However, there is no need to enumerate all the irregularities here. In a word, whatever may be called by the term "superstition" is that which is superfluous, not essential to salvation, devised by hypocrites only for their own interest, beguiling the simple people, and like snowdrifts, hindering passage along the right path of truth. All this is incorporated in the present survey as a general evil since it can be found among all classes. Only several examples are given here, so that on the basis of these, others also may be watched for.

This has been the first point concerning common matters.

The second point, also concerning common matters, as was previously mentioned, has to do with examining whether we have instruction suitable for Christian improvement.

For although it is known that Holy Scripture itself contains all the laws and commandments needed for our salvation (according to the Apostle, 2 Timothy 3: "All Scripture is inspired by God and useful for teaching, for reproving, for correcting, for instructing in justice; that the man of God may be perfect, equipped for every good work" [27]), nevertheless, since few are able to read books, and few are able to gather from those who are literate everything from Scripture that is essential for salvation, the guidance of competent men is therefore required. Accordingly the pastoral office was established by God, so that, from Holy Scripture, it would teach the flock entrusted to it.

However, despite the large number of people in the Russian Church, there are few presbyters who can preach from memory the dogmas and laws of Holy Scripture. The ultimate need is to have some short booklets, clear and comprehensible to ordinary people, in which is included all that is appropriate for the instruction of the people. Those booklets can then be read in parts during weekdays and holydays in the churches before the people.

Although there is a sufficient number of such books as the *Homologia,* or *Orthodox Confession of Faith,*[28] and also exegetical discourses and homilies of certain holy teachers, this instruction nevertheless is not practical for all, especially the common people. For the book, *Orthodox Confession of Faith,* is not small, and because of that, it is difficult to implant in the memory of simple people. It is not written in the vernacular, and because of that, it is to a large extent not intelligible to the simple. Likewise the books of the great teachers, Chrysostom,[29] Theophylact,[30] and others, are written in Greek and are intelligible only in that language. Their translation into Slavonic has become turbid and only with effort can be understood even by educated persons, while it is absolutely incomprehensible to simple ignoramuses. And on top of that, the exegetical di-

dactic discourses contain many lofty theological mysteries. Likewise
they say much that at the time it may have been appropriate to say,
according to the inclinations of various peoples and according to the
circumstances of their time, but which an uneducated person could
not use for his benefit now. However, it is fitting often to point out
to the common people that which is most obligatory for everyone
generally and for each one individually, according to his calling.
Even now it is impossible to have these books in all the village
churches, but just in city churches, and then only in wealthy ones.
Accordingly it is necessary to treat human infirmity by another
method. One reaches the following conclusion: if all were to understand the most important dogmas of our faith, and the vision of
what our salvation is as arranged by God, and if they could understand the commandments of God, to shun evil and to do good, then
this would be adequate instruction for them. However, if someone
even with such knowledge were to remain corrupt, then he would
himself be without reply before God and not the pastoral officer,
faithfully serving to bring about his salvation.

Accordingly it is necessary to compose three small booklets. The
first on the most important soteriological dogmas of our faith; likewise on the commandments of God, contained in the Decalogue.

The second on the individual obligations of every class.

The third is to be of such a kind, in which there shall be collected
clear sermons from various holy teachers, as on the most important
dogmas, so even more on sins and virtues, and particularly on the
obligations of every class. The first and second booklets are to draw
their arguments from Holy Scripture itself, but are to be brief and
intelligible to all. The third, from the holy fathers, shall expound
upon that which is in the first and second.[31]

The reading from those booklets shall proceed expeditiously in
this order. On a Sunday or holy day, at matins, a small part shall be
read from the first booklet, and during another sequence, a part
from the second booklet. On the same day, in the mass, a selection
shall be read from the third booklet on the subject read about at
matins. Thus the one and the same lesson, heard at matins and re-
iterated in the mass, can be better retained in the memory of the listen-
ers.

All those parts that are read shall be so divided that all three booklets can be read in one-quarter of a year. For, thus, the people will hear all their needed instructions four times a year and will be able to remember well what is heard.

Furthermore it should be made known that children also will be able to study the first and second booklets from the beginning of their instruction in the alphabet.

Although those booklets are to be three in number, yet all three can be included in one small book, so that they may be purchased at small expense and used not only in the churches but in the homes of all interested persons without difficulty.[32]

Matters Pertaining to Bishops
Following the Above Discussion on Common Matters,
There Now Is Set Forth Something on What the
Particular Obligations of Bishops, Presbyters,
Monks, and Others Are

Here is what should be known with regard to bishops.

1. Bishops are obliged to hold various councils, ecumenical and national, among themselves. Whatever is commanded in them, as obligatory for their own rank as for the entire clergy, shall be well known, and this cannot be done without diligent and frequent reading.

2. They are particularly obliged to know the degrees of lineal and collateral kinship, and who may be allowed to marry and who may not, either according to the commandment of God, in the Book of Leviticus, chapter 18, or according to the Church, in the patristic and imperial canons. They should attend to this themselves and not delegate it to someone else, even though a person experienced in this may be available to them.

3. Just as the first, so also their second aforementioned obligation cannot be well understood without diligent reading; but whether everyone will be eager to read is not known. Accordingly there shall be presented to all bishops an ukase from the Spiritual College that each one, at his refection, shall have the readings of the canons that are pertinent to him. As an exception, this may sometimes be waived on major holy days, or in the presence of notable guests, or for some other appropriate reason.

4. If some difficult matter arises and a bishop is perplexed about

what to do, then, first, he shall write about it, requesting advice, to the other bishop in closest proximity, or to some other who is experienced. Later, if he still remains unsatisfied, he should write to the Spiritual College in the capital, Saint Petersburg, clearly, summarily, and accurately.

5. There are canons that forbid bishops to linger for a long time away from their eparchy (which anyone can verify from the conciliar book). If an unavoidable exigency intervenes that keeps him outside the eparchy, as, for example, the regular period of service in the capital or some other appropriate reason, or likewise, if a serious infirmity occurs that in great measure prevents the conduct of affairs (for such an indisposed person is comparable to one who is absent), in such an instance a bishop is obliged, in addition to his ordinary domestic administrators, to appoint for the conduct of affairs some intelligent man of honorable background, an archimandrite or hegumen, adding as an aid to him several other intelligent monks or priests. They shall inform him, the bishop who is absent, of important matters in writing, and to him who is indisposed, they shall report orally, if he can listen notwithstanding his infirmity. If matters arise that those administrators are unable to resolve, then they shall write about them to the Spiritual College, as was stated above in reference to bishops themselves.

6. Bishops shall issue a similar command and ukase to their subordinate archimandrites, hegumens, superiors, and parish priests in the event that serious illness befalls them or an important reason keeps them from their monastery or parish.

7. When a bishop, because of extreme old age or some incurable disease, grows exceedingly feeble, without hope of better health, so that it becomes completely impossible for him to discharge his obligations, in that event, a bishop, over and above the aforementioned extraordinary administrators who have been appointed in his place, must render a complete written report to the Spiritual College. Should a bishop, however, not desire to write about himself, then, nevertheless, his administrators must write about him. In the Spiritual College it shall be decided what to do, whether to assign some administrator to that eparchy or to install a new bishop.

8. A bishop is obliged to observe that which he promised with an oath to observe at his consecration, that is, in reference to monks, that they do not wander aimlessly, that unnecessary churches, with

no people, are not built, that false miracles are not contrived for
holy icons. Likewise he shall be well on the watch for squallers,[33]
noncertified corpses,[34] and all other suchlike.

To do all that more efficiently, a bishop must order in all cities
that stewards,[35] or ecclesiastical superintendents,[36] especially appointed for that purpose, just as if they were spiritual fiscals, are to
oversee all those things and report to him, the bishop. If something
like that appears anywhere, whoever desires to conceal it shall do so
under penalty of the ban.

9. Highly useful for the reform of the Church is this, that each
bishop have in his house, or attached to his house, a school for the
children of priests, or of others, who have been assigned there as
likely prospects for a priestly vocation. In that school there shall be
an intelligent and honorable teacher, who shall teach the children
not only to read books properly, clearly, and accurately (which, although it is needful, is nevertheless still not enough), but should
teach them to read and to understand, and if possible, to recite from
memory the first two booklets mentioned above: the one on the dogmas of the faith, and the other on the obligations of all classes,
when such booklets will be published. The student who is utterly
stupid, or although intelligent, is depraved, intractable, and insuper-
ably lazy, shall be, after sufficient probation, released from the
school and deprived of all hope of the priesthood.

10. Only such students as are placed in an episcopal school
(when already, with God's help, a sufficient number of them will
appear) shall be elevated to the priesthood, or whoever among them
chooses the monastic life, then into the archimandrites or hegumens,
except for him who is blocked by some important reason. If, however, a bishop installs into the priesthood, or into monastic life,
someone who has not been taught in that kind of school, having
passed over without sufficient reason one who had been thus taught,
then he shall be subject to such punishment as shall be determined
by the Spiritual College.

11. Lest there be complaints from the parents of students regarding the high cost of the teacher, of purchasing books, and of provid-
ing for their sons, studying far from their home, it is fitting that the
students be fed and taught gratis and with the bishops' books available.

That this might be accomplished, the following decision has been made: from the most prominent monasteries in an eparchy, a one-twentieth part of all kinds of grain shall be taken; and from church lands, wherever they may be, a one-thirtieth part of all kinds of grain shall be taken. As many persons as that grain will provide with subsistence and other needs (clothing excepted), such shall be the number of students, with the necessary servants.

A bishop shall furnish the teacher, or teachers, with food and prestimony from the episcopal treasury, as the Spiritual College shall determine according to local evaluation.

12. Such contributions by monasteries and church lands will cause no great poverty for the churches and monasteries, if only their domestic economy is good and true. Every year they shall give the bishop information as to what amount of every grain has been harvested; and the bishop shall supervise where the grain goes that exceeds all the necessary requirements by its abundance.

For that purpose there shall be in the Spiritual College books of revenues and expenditures for all the most prominent monasteries in Russia. By expenditures is here meant those that are customary and permanent, not extraordinary or occasional such as for necessary construction, etc.

Nevertheless, for such extraordinary expenditures, it is fitting in the College to make estimates regarding the needs of each monastery as against the revenues.

13. Lest the bishops begin to complain, as though it were a hardship for them to pay the teacher or teachers, it shall be commanded them that they not retain superfluous servants and not construct unnecessary buildings [37] (but only useful buildings, for example, windmills, etc.); likewise, that they not accumulate sacerdotal vestments, and any apparel, over and above the proper requirement of their dignity.

However, for the better administration of everything, the books of episcopal revenues shall be kept in the Spiritual College. More about teachers and teaching will be found below in its place.

14. Every bishop shall observe moderation with regard to his dignity and not esteem it highly as a thing of consequence, for as one reads in Scripture, it is the work that is great, without any corresponding illustrious honor. The Apostle, confuting the opinion of the Corinthians, who prided themselves on their pastors, says that the pastoral vocation has all its success and fruit from God Himself,

acting in human hearts. "I have planted," he says, "Apollos watered, but God has given the growth." [38] Wherefore he concludes that, for this growth, no praise is remaining to man. "So neither he who plants nor he who waters is anything, but only God who gives the growth." [39] And he therein calls pastors God's servants and stewards of His mysteries only if in that vocation they remain trustworthy.[40] For the task of pastors is only external, to preach, to instruct, to interdict in season and out of season, and to perform the rites of the Holy Mysteries. There is also the inner task of God alone, acting by His grace through the word and sacramental functions of the pastors, as though invisibly through an instrument, to turn hearts toward repentance and to a renewal of life.

[15] [41] Accordingly, this is set forth to temper the highly excessive glory of bishops. They should not be led about under the arms as long as they are in good health, and the brethren should not bow to the ground before them. For those who bow spread themselves on the ground willfully and impudently, even falsely, in order to impetrate undeserved rank for themselves and thereby hide their fury and lawlessness.[42] The truth is that the pastoral vocation, if it is but carried out even only externally, is nevertheless not a small thing, for it is God's mission. And God commands, "Let the presbyters who rule well be held worthy of double honor, especially those who labor in the word and in teaching" (1 Tim. 5).[43] Yet this honor is a modest one, and is not to be exaggerated or thought of as being almost equal to that of the Tsar; and pastors themselves are not to seek even a modest honor and extort it from subordinates, but they are to be satisfied with such as is freely proffered.

16. From the foregoing, it follows that a bishop should not be harsh and precipitate, but forbearing and judicious in exercising his binding power, that is, in excommunicating and anathematizing. The Lord gave this authority for building, and not for destroying, says the Apostle (1 Cor. 10).[44] And the intention of that same teacher of peoples was to deliver a Corinthian, clearly a sinner, to Satan for the destruction of the flesh, so that the soul might be saved (1 Cor. 5).[45] For this authority to be used properly, it is necessary to observe two things:

First, what offense is deserving of such great punishment.

The other, how a bishop is to mete out that punishment.

The offense may be determined by this reasoning: if someone

manifestly blasphemes God's name, or Holy Scripture, or the Church, or is clearly a sinner who is unashamed of his acts and, even more, boasts of them, or does not go to confession and does not receive the Holy Eucharist for more than a year without good reason, or does anything else with clear vilification and mockery of God's law, such a one, who remains stubborn and haughty after repeated punishment, shall be adjudged as deserving that great penalty. Not merely for sin is he subject to anathema, but for the clear and haughty contempt of God's judgment and of Church authority, with great tempting of weak brethren, and because he exudes from himself the stench of godlessness.

This shall be the proper procedure or conduct of the matter.

First, a bishop shall send that person's confessor to him to explain to him his offense privately, with humility and with exhortation that he cease his activity. Whereas by obvious and prideful sin he has tried the Church, the confessor shall undertake to implore him that, on the nearest holyday, he ought to bring repentance to his spiritual father, accept the penance, and receive the Holy Eucharist in front of the people, so that his transformation may be made manifest and the scandal expunged, and that he ought not to return to his abominations. And if, having heard this, the guilty person submits and fulfills what is directed, the bishop has won his brother and there is nothing more to be done.

However, if that mission should be in vain, then a bishop, after some time, shall summon him to himself, in honor, with a request, and shall likewise repeat the instruction to him secretly, in the presence only of the single confessor who had previously gone to him. If he obeys, a brother is won.

However, if the person summoned does not go to the bishop, then the bishop shall send to him that same confessor together with several other persons, ecclesiastical and laic, most especially the friends of that person, to exhort him in the same manner as at first. Here, if he submits and acts according to the instruction, the matter is resolved.

Yet, if notwithstanding even this he remains obdurate and haughty, then once again the same kind of delegation can be renewed.

If all goes for nought, then the bishop shall direct the archdeacon to make an announcement on a holyday to the people in these or similar words: "The person, known to you as, (saying the name), by such obvious transgression expressly tries the Church and appears as a contemner of God's wrath, and he has rejected with vilification the pastoral instruction that was repeated to him more than once. Accordingly your pastor, (saying the name), paternally begs your love, that all will pray to Merciful God for that sinner, that He soften his hardheartedness, instill in him a clean heart, and incline him to repentance. Whoever has the closest communication with him exhort and implore him, each one individually and with others all together, in all earnestness, that he repent; and inform him that, if he remains unregenerate and contumacious until such a time (the time shall be fixed according to a determination), he shall fall under the ban of the Church."

If now, even after this, the criminal remains obdurate and stubborn, the bishop shall not yet then resort to anathema, but shall beforehand write to the Spiritual College on how all that occurred. After having received consent in writing from the College, he shall publicly pronounce the sinner's anathema, having composed this or a similar formula, or model, and having commanded the archdeacon to read it in the church before the people: "Whereas the person known to you as, (saying the name), by such-and-such a manifest crime against God's Law, has tried the Church and has rejected numerous pastoral exhortations leading him to repentance, and finally, having scorned his expulsion from the Church if he does not repent, which was announced in the hearing of the people, remains even now in his hardheartedness and offers no hope for his regeneration: wherefore our pastor, in consonance with Christ's commandment, by the authority given to him by that same Christ, Our Lord, bans him from the Christian community, and like a useless organ, excises him from the body of Christ's Church, announcing as regards him to all true believers that he is herewith not to share in God's gifts, gained for us by the blood of our Savior and Lord, Jesus Christ, until he truly repents from the heart. Consequently he is forbidden and not permitted entrance into any church, most especially for the Holy and Terrifying Mystery of the Eucharist and the other Holy Mysteries; and he cannot be a participant in ecclesiastical ceremonies, as in church, so in his own house and in any other place. If he should enter a church secretly, or even openly, but by force, then he shall be subject to greater judgment, and even more if he dares, through guile or force, to receive the Holy Mysteries. Priests shall, by all possible means, deny him access into church; and if they are not able to impede him because of his force, then, except for the liturgy,[46] they shall stop any church service until he withdraws. Likewise priests shall not go to him [47] with prayer, benediction, and the Holy Mysteries, lest they be divested of their ecclesiastical dignity.

"Let it be known to all that only he, (saying the same), personally is subject to this anathema, and not his wife, children, or others of his household,[48] unless they desire to imitate his malevolence, and haughtily and openly dare to reproach God's Church for this proscription that has been imposed on him."

This or some other model for anathematization that in the judgment of the College should be prescribed shall, after the reading, be attached to the church doors, either those of the cathedral alone or of all the churches in that eparchy, whichever the College shall decide.

Later, if the excommunicate comes to his senses and desires to repent, then he himself must, or if he is not able to himself, then through other honest persons, make his repentance to the bishop publicly in church with all humility and ask for remission, with the confession of his sin and arrogant contumacy. Then the bishop shall ask him these questions: Whether truly and for the sake of forgiveness of sins, fearing God's wrath and beseeching God's mercy, he repents; whether he believes that the authority of pastors to loose and to bind is not trifling, but is mighty, efficacious, and terrifying; and whether he promises that he shall henceforth be an obedient son of the Church and shall not undertake to contemn the authority of pastors. According to his answers, delivered in the hearing of all the people, the bishop shall direct him to trust firmly God's mercy, shown to the repenting sinner through the Savior's death, and shall read over him the remission of the punishment. Thereupon, having instructed him on the amendment of his life (which lesson can be composed later), he shall prescribe to him some designated feast day for going to receive the Holy Eucharist, after confessing to his spiritual father.

However, if the excommunicate, not having repented, undertakes further to abuse the church anathema, or to do harm to the bishop or the other clergy, then the bishop shall send a petition about it to the Spiritual College, and the College, having searched out the truth, shall with insistence request a judgment by the appropriate civil authority or from His Tsarist Majesty himself.

This, however, shall the College most strongly prescribe to the bishops, that they not perform either anathemas or remissions for the sake of their own gain or any other personal interest, and that they strive in such an important matter not for themselves but for the Lord Jesus.

This procedure is the proper one in such a matter, consonant with the word of God and not subject to suspicion.

But this passage was about anathema, which is malediction, a punishment similar to death. Through anathema, a person is severed from the Mystical Body of Christ, that is, from the Church, and because of that, does not remain a Christian, but is alienated from the legacy of all the blessings gained for us by the Savior's death. Thus it appears from the words of God: "Let him be to thee as the heathen and the publican,[49] and it is fitting to deliver such a one over to Satan," [50] and others similar to these.

There is in Holy Church a lesser punishment, called minor excommunication or interdict. This occurs when the Church does not pronounce outright the sinner's anathema and does not eject him from Christ's flock, but only restrains him by excluding him from association with true believers in common prayers. It does not allow him to enter God's temples, and for a certain time, forbids him communion in the Holy Mysteries. Briefly speaking, through anathema a person is like one who has been killed; but through minor excommunication or interdict, he is like one who has been placed under arrest.

There are examples of both these punishments, the greater and the lesser, in the Church councils, where anathema was uttered against heretics. However, transgressors of the councils' canons were punished by minor excommunication.

The offense deserving of the lesser punishment, that is, of minor excommunication, is some great and manifest sin, but not the very greatest obvious transgression, which was already discussed above. For example, when someone is clearly given to disorderly conduct, for a long time absents himself from church-singing, or does not ask for forgiveness when he has openly offended or dishonored an honest person, then a bishop, having instructed such offenders himself, or through a confessor, that they are to bring public repentance, can restrain them by minor excommunication, if they should not desire to comply and provided that they do not display intolerable arrogance and contumacy, without his resorting to those solemn announcements through the archdeacon, but only publishing the offense of the criminal and his excommunication in a written notice.

In such a matter, a bishop is not required to render a complete report to the College for approval, but he is free and empowered to carry it into execution himself, except that he do this not through passion, but through diligent investigation. For if he excommunicates someone innocent, and that one seeks judgment against him in the College, the bishop shall be punished according to the decision of the Spiritual College.

17. In Article 8 above, each bishop was directed to observe that obligatory commandments are kept in his eparchy by presbyters, monks, etc., and that, for this, he is to have spiritual fiscals. However, this is not enough, for even those fiscals, as friends of their benefactors or through bribery, conceal much. Accordingly it is fitting for a bishop to tour and visit his eparchy yearly, or once every two years. In this regard there is, besides many others, the great example of Apostle Paul, as appears in Acts, chapter 14, verses 21–22, and Acts, chapter 15, verse 36; Romans, chapter 1, verses 11–12; 1 Corinthians, chapter 4, verse 12; [51] 1 Thessalonians, chapter 3, verse 2; and 1 Thessalonians, chapter 3, verse 10.

For improving this visit, the following regulations are applicable.

(1) Summertime appears to be more suitable for the visit than winter. This is because the bishop himself and the visited churches will not spend so much in the summer as in winter on sustenance and other requirements. Hay is not needed and there is little demand for firewood. Bread, fish, and fodder for horses are cheaper. Furthermore a bishop can stay for a longer time in a tent in a field not far from the city, so as not to trouble the clergy or the citizens for lodging, especially when the city is poor.

(2) On the second or third day after his arrival, a bishop, having gathered the urban and village presbyters, shall celebrate the Holy Liturgy, and after the Liturgy, with all the priests, he shall perform a prayer service for the health and victory of the Most Powerful Monarch, for the regeneration and welfare of the churches, for the

return of the schismatics, for seasonable weather, for an abundance of the fruits of the earth, etc. A special canon, containing all the desiderata, shall be compiled.

(3) Then, after the completion of this service, he shall deliver a didactic sermon to the priesthood and the people on true repentance and the obligations of every, and especially the priestly, class. Therein he shall add an exhortation that whoever has any spiritual needs or has perplexing moral questions on his conscience present them to him; likewise, if anywhere there is seen something amiss among the church personnel, etc. However, since not every bishop is able to put together a clear exhortation, it is therefore fitting to compose such a sermon in the Spiritual College, so that the bishops may read it in the visited churches.

(4) A bishop can secretly inquire, from the lesser churchmen and whoever else appears suitable, how the presbyters and deacons live. Although it is not called for to believe hurriedly everyone's delation, nevertheless, at least a good basis will have appeared for investigation and correction.

(5) Until a bishop has settled the matters that have been reported, he shall not invite guests to visit him, and if invited, he shall not go to visit others, lest he be flattered by entertainment or at least cast upon himself the suspicion that he judges with partiality because of the pleasure given to him.

(6) If a matter arises that requires a long time because of the unavailability of witnesses or some other hindrance, then, having recorded that matter, he shall postpone it for settlement in his own house. For he should not visit long in any one place, and there should remain time for him to visit the entire eparchy.

(7) Should a bishop desire to invite guests, then let him arrange that entire entertainment out of his own funds and not impose an assessment on the priesthood or the monasteries. And he may not excuse himself by his poverty, for it is not through duty but through his own free will that he invites or does not invite guests.

(8) Other matters and activities, as of the clergy, so also of members of the parish, may be concealed from a bishop even though they are known to the people; and such are to be secretly and artfully ascertained. However, this cannot be concealed: whether a priest on holydays reads the instructional booklets concerning which there was a statement given above. If one does not read them out of lazi-

ness, he is to be punished in front of the other priests, according to the finding.

(9) A bishop shall inquire of the clergy and other persons whether superstitious practices are carried on anywhere. Are squallers to be found? Is there anyone who, for ill-gotten gain, displays false miracles connected with icons, wells, springs, etc.? And he shall forbid such nonsense, with the threat of malediction against recalcitrants who resist.

(10) It is better to ask priests and laymen in the cities and villages about the administration and conduct of nearby monasteries (wherever there are any) rather than to spend time making inquiries in those same monasteries.

(11) So that a bishop does not forget what he is supposed to look for in the visited churches and monasteries, he shall have with him for that purpose a list of the monastic and priestly responsibilities, which are to be found below.

(12) A bishop is obliged firmly to command his servitors that, in the visited cities and monasteries, they remain orderly and sober, and that they not create a disturbance; especially that they not importune the monks and priests for food and drink and excess horse fodder; further, that they particularly do not dare to rob, under penalty of severe punishment. For episcopal servants usually are gluttonous beasts; and where they see their bishop's authority, there, with great arrogance and shamelessness, like the Tatars, they embark upon pillage.

(13) Let every bishop know, of whatever rank he may be, whether an ordinary bishop, an archbishop, or a metropolitan, that he is subordinate to the Spiritual College as to the supreme authority. He shall obey its ukases, shall be subject to its judgment, and shall be content with its decisions. Accordingly, if one has a grievance against his brother, another bishop, having been wronged by him, it is fitting that he not take revenge himself, either by aspersions, or by tales of his sins, even if they be true, or by the instigation of certain powerful ecclesiastical or lay persons. Most especially let him not venture to anathematize the unfriendly bishop. Let him put forward his wrongs in a report to the Spiritual College and seek judgment for himself there.[52]

(14) Furthermore any archimandrite, hegumen, superior, parish priest, and likewise, even deacons and any other members of the

clergy, may freely and voluntarily seek judgment from the Spiritual College against his bishop if one should be greatly wronged by him in something. Likewise, if someone is not content with a judgment of his bishop, he shall be free to originate an appeal, that is, transfer the matter to the judgment of the Spiritual College; and a bishop must allow this freedom to such petitioners and plaintiffs against himself. He shall not detain them, threaten them, or, in their absence while at the Spiritual College, seal up or loot their houses.

However, lest this furnish many persons with reason for audacity and contumacy toward their pastors, the Spiritual College shall prescribe not inconsiderable punishments for those who would venture to sacrifice their pastors through false delation or without cause would originate an appeal from a bishop's judgment to the judgment of the Spiritual College.

(15) Finally, each bishop shall be obliged twice a year (or however the College may prescribe) to send reports to the College, that is, accounts of the condition and behavior of his eparchy, whether everything is well or whether there is some irregularity that he is unable to resolve. However, even if everything is well, then nevertheless a bishop is obliged to notify the College that, glory be to God, all is well. But if he gives notice that all is well, and from elsewhere it appears that something superstitious, or something obviously odious to God, is occurring in his eparchy and that the bishop, knowing that, conceals it without informing the College, then the College shall summon him personally before it for judgment. Upon sufficient presentation of evidence, he shall be subject to punishment, such as shall be prescribed.

Teachers and Students in Educational Institutions So Also Church Preachers

It is known to the whole world how inadequate and weak was the Russian army when it did not have proper training and how incomparably its numbers increased and how it became great and formidable beyond expectation when Our Most Powerful Monarch, His Tsarist Majesty, Peter I, instructed it with most excellent regulations. The same is to be appreciated as regards architecture, medicine, political government, and all other affairs.

Especially is this to be appreciated as regards the administration of the Church: When the light of learning is extinguished there cannot be good order in the Church; there cannot be but disorder and superstitions deserving of much ridicule. in addition to dissension and most senseless heresies.

Foolishly do many say that education is responsible for heresy. For, quite apart from ancient heretics, who were bedeviled by arrogant folly and not by learning, the Valentinians,[53] Manicheans,[54] Cathars,[55] Eutychians,[56] Donatists,[57] and others, whose follies are related by Irenaeus,[58] Epiphanius,[59] Augustine,[60] Theodoret,[61] and others, have not our Russian schismatics become as severely possessed through coarseness and ignorance? And although heresiarchs may arise from among learned persons, such as were Arius,[62] Nestorius, and some others, yet heresy was born in them not through learning, but through a false understanding of the Holy Scriptures, and grew and strengthened out of rancor and pride. which did not allow them to change their rash opinion even contrary to their conscience upon realization of the truth. Although from their teachings they had the ability to develop sophisms, that is, specious arguments from their speculation, nevertheless, whoever would attribute this evil simply to learning would be constrained to say that, when a physician overdoses someone with poison, medical science is responsible for it, and when a trained soldier cunningly and forcibly brings about a defeat, that military science is to blame. If we look throughout history, as through a telescope, upon past ages, we shall find everything to have been worse in dark times than in times enlightened by learning. Not before the year 400 did bishops affect such a superior manner as they kindled afterwards, especially the bishops of Constantinople and Rome. Before that time, there had been learning, but later it became impoverished. If learning were deleterious to the Church or to the state, then the most eminent Christian personages would not study, and would forbid others to learn. Instead, we see that all our early teachers studied not only Holy Scriptures, but even natural philosophy. In addition to many others, the most renowned pillars of the Church advocate study even of the physical world: namely, Basil the Great,[63] in his discourse to young students; Chrysostom,[64] in his books on monasticism; Gregory the Theologian,[65] in his discourses against Julian the Apostate. But much could be said in a special treatise on this topic alone.

Thus, learning is beneficial and basic for every good, as of the fatherland, so also of the Church, just like the root and the seed and the foundation. Only it must be most carefully watched that the learning be good and sound.

There is also learning that is unworthy of the name; nevertheless it is regarded as genuine learning by people who, although intelligent, are ignorant in this respect.

Many customarily ask: "What courses did that person pursue?" And when they hear that he studied rhetoric, philosophy, and theology, they admire that person highly on account of those names alone, in which they often err. For not everyone learns well even from good teachers, sometimes because of mental dullness, sometimes because of their own laziness; and this is especially true when the teacher is little, or even less than little, experienced in his work.

It is appropriate to observe that in all Europe from the year 500 to the year 1400, that is, for nine hundred years, nearly all studies were in great destitution and want of competence, so that we see the very best writers of that period possessed of great mental acuity, but we do not see great illumination. After the year 1400, there began to appear most inquisitive, and because of that, most highly versed, teachers. Little by little, many academies acquired a very great capability, almost as considerable as in the ancient Augustan age. Many educational institutions, nevertheless, remained in the former mire, so that they had only the names of rhetoric and philosophy and the other studies, but not the pursuit thereof. The reasons for that are diverse and for the sake of brevity are not reviewed here.

Persons who have partaken of such, so to speak, spectral and delusive learning are sometimes more foolish than uneducated ones. As they are very truly benighted, they fancy themselves to be accomplished, and assuming that they have learned everything there is to know, they do not wish to learn more, nor do they even think of reading books. Conversely, a person enlightened with genuine learning never reaches satiation in his knowledge; rather, he never ceases to learn even though he should live as long as Methuselah.

It is most deplorable that such sciolists are not only useless, but are extremely harmful to their colleagues, to the fatherland, and to the Church. Before the authorities they cringe beyond measure, but slyly, in order thus to steal their favor and to insinuate themselves into an honorable post. They detest people of equal rank; and if someone is praised for his erudition, they strive by all possible means to slight and to disparage him before the people and with the authorities. They incline toward rebellion, entertaining high hopes. When they theologize, they cannot but enter into heresy, for they readily blunder in speaking on account of their ignorance; and in no way do they desire to change their expressed opinion, lest they betray themselves, that they do not know everything. But discerning men have confirmed among themselves this saying: The mark of a wise man is the ability to change his opinion.

It has been judged as beneficial to propose that, if His Tsarist Majesty desires to found an Academy, the Spiritual College should deliberate on what teachers to appoint initially and what model of instruction to show them, so that state expenditure may not go for nought and so that there may not be emptiness deserving of ridicule instead of the expected advantage.

The following regulations are applicable on how to proceed circumspectly and skillfully in this:

1. Initially a great number of teachers is unsuitable, but in the first year, one or two shall be enough. These shall teach grammar, that is, to know correctly the Latin language, or Greek, or both languages.

2. Entering upon higher studies, a greater number of teachers shall be added in the next year, and the third year, and later, while the first year's subject shall be continued for new students.

3. Everyone who desires to be a teacher shall be tested in his subject: for example, when it is desired to find out whether one is proficient in Latin, he shall be directed to translate a Russian composition into Latin and, likewise, to translate a Latin work by some renowned author in that language into Russian. Knowledgeable persons shall be directed to inspect and examine his translations, and forthwith, it will become evident whether he is accomplished or average or lower than that or quite without value. There are, for other studies, appropriate tests that can be specially compiled.

4. Even though one shows himself incompetent in a required subject, but it is apparent that he is intelligent and that he obviously did not succeed in it because of laziness or because of a poor teacher, such a one shall be directed to study, for half a year or a year, under authors versed in that subject if he aspires to be a teacher. This is to be done only because of the scarcity of people, and it is better not to rely upon such persons.

5. Capable teachers who have been appointed shall be ordered ini-

tially to tell their students briefly but clearly what the purpose of the present study is, of grammar, for example, of rhetoric, logic, etc., and what we desire to accomplish through this or some other study, so that the students might see the shore toward which they are sailing, acquire better motivation, and ascertain their daily progress as well as their shortcomings.

6. In every subject, the foremost authors shall be selected, those who are recognized in famous academies: as a specific example, in Paris, at the command [66] of King Louis XIV, there is a Latin grammar [67] so short, yet so completely inclusive, that it is possible to expect an intelligent student to learn that language thoroughly in one year, where with us there are few who grasp it in five, or even six, years. This becomes evident when a student who has graduated from philosophy or theology is unable to translate even middle style Latin. Thus, after the best authors in grammar, rhetoric, and other studies have been selected, as has been described, they shall be turned over to the Academy, and it shall be ordered that classes be taught through their guidance and not that of others.

7. In theology, it shall be specifically ordered that the main dogmas of our faith and God's Law are to be taught. A teacher of theology should read the Holy Scriptures and should study the canons on how to know the real, true meaning and significance of the Scriptures, and he should strengthen all dogmas by the testimony of the Scriptures. To assist in that task, he should read sedulously the books of the holy fathers, especially those fathers who, struggling against dissident heresies, wrote diligently about dogmas on account of controversies within the Church. For there are early teachers who wrote about particular dogmas, one about this and another about that. For example: on the mystery of the Trinity, Gregory Nazianzus, in his five theological discourses,[68] and Augustine, in books on the Trinity and on the divinity of the Son of God, besides others; [69] Athanasius the Great, in five books against the Arians on the divinity of the Holy Ghost; [70] Basil the Great, in five books against Eunomius; [71] Cyril of Alexandria, in five books against Nestorius on the hypostasis of Christ; [72] on the two natures in Christ, sufficient is the one epistle of Leo, pope of Rome, to Flavian, patriarch of Constantinople; [73] Augustine, in many books against the Pelagians on original sin and God's grace,[74] etc. Likewise, in this regard, the proceedings

and discussions of the ecumenical and local councils are exceedingly useful. With such teachers, in addition to the Holy Scriptures, theological instruction will not be useless. Although a teacher of theology may seek aid from the most recent teachers of other faiths, he must nevertheless not learn from them or trust their stories, but only accept their guidance as to whatever arguments they draw from the Scriptures and from the early teachers. This is so especially with dogmas in which they are accordant with us. Still, their arguments are not to be believed lightly, but shall be examined whether there is such a tenor in the Scriptures or in the patristic books and whether it has the same meaning as they admit. For those gentlemen frequently lie and adduce what has never existed. Often they pervert the true message. As an example, the following passage, in which Our Lord speaks to Peter, will suffice: "But I have prayed for you, that your faith may not fail." [75] Here Peter is spoken to personally, the reference is to Peter as an individual, but the Latins shift this to their pope, inferring therefrom that the pope cannot err in matters of faith even if he should desire. A teacher of theology therefore must instruct not according to foreign stories, but according to his own understanding, and occasionally, having selected a special time, he is to show evidence to his students in the books, so that they themselves may be convinced and not doubt whether their teacher speaks the truth or falsehood.

8. Here, by way of incidental advice, it is mentioned that an adequate library is requisite in conjunction with classes. For without a library, an academy is as without a soul. But it is possible to purchase an adequate library for two thousand rubles.

A library is to be, every day and hour, unrestricted for use by teachers, provided only that they not take the books to their cells, but read them in the library room itself. But for students and other interested persons, the library shall be open during set days and hours.

Those who know the language should, as in duty bound, go to the library during special hours and days besides the other times that are fixed for going and those in which they go out of their own interests. A teacher should ask each of his students what author he is reading, what he has read, and what he has written; and if he has not understood something, the teacher should explain it to him. This is extremely beneficial and quickly, as it were, transforms a person completely even though he previously may have possessed coarse habits.

9. Turning to scholastic studies, it seems to be extremely advantageous when certain lessons, two or three together, can be presented in a single hour as one subject. For example, when teaching grammar, a teacher can jointly with it teach both geography and history, for according to the rules of grammar, it is necessary to do exercises, to learn through translations from my language into that language which I am studying and, conversely, from that language into my language. It is then possible to direct students to translate, in part, geography or history, either secular alone or ecclesiastical, or for a change, both those studies.

Since to read history without an understanding of geography is like walking on the street blindfolded, it is therefore a sound suggestion that the year scheduled for grammar should be divided in two parts and, during the first half-year, that grammar should be taught together with geography, designating a special day of the week on which the teacher will show on a map the circles, planispheres, and the universal situation of the world. It would be even better to do this on a globe and so to teach the students that they might be able to point out with a finger when someone asks them: Where is Asia? Where is Africa? Where is Europe? In what direction from us does America lie? Likewise, about the states separately: Where is Egypt? Where is China? Where is Portugal? etc. The other half-year should be devoted to exercises in translating universal history, or even a condensed history, provided only that the author selected uses pure Latin, as does the historian Justin [76] and others who can be looked into later.

This is extremely beneficial, as students will acquire great enthusiasm for learning when the dull study of language is revealed to them through the so lively study of the world and through knowledge of the passing events in the world. Swiftly will coarseness fall away from them, and while still, as it were, almost at the school's shore, they will find not a few valuable wares.

10. The following appears to be a good program of instruction: (1) Grammar, jointly with geography and history. (2) Arithmetic and geometry. (3) Logic or dialectics, a single study with two names. (4) Rhetoric, jointly with, or separately from, the study of

poetry. (5) Physics, adding thereto a brief metaphysics. (6) Pufendorf's abridged politics: [77] if considered applicable, this can be added to dialectics. (7) Theology.

The first six shall take a year each, and theology, two years. For although each subject, except dialectics and grammar, is extensive, in class it is nevertheless necessary to treat them briefly, and only the most important parts. Whoever receives such good guidance will afterward obtain further improvement through his own reading and practice. The Greek and Hebrew languages shall be allocated a set time among the other subjects (if there are teachers).

11. Diligent persons, whose erudition and achievements are already known, shall be chosen as rector and prefect. The Spiritual College shall direct them to be careful in their work, with this warning, that, should studies proceed not in accordance with the program and without due speed, then they themselves shall be subject to judgment in the Spiritual College. Accordingly they must watch that the teachers go to school and that they teach as it is fitting. The rector and prefect must visit two classes a week, and the following week, another two, and thus the others in turn. When they arrive in a class, the teacher shall instruct before them, and they shall listen for at least half an hour. Likewise, they shall test the students with questions, whether they know what they are at that point supposed to know.

12. If some teacher appears in violation of Academy regulations and is unyielding to the rector's instruction, the rector shall report him to the Spiritual College. After investigation, he shall be dismissed or punished in accordance with the finding.

13. Fiscals can be assigned to watch that everything in the Academy proceeds in an orderly manner.

14. The following provision concerns students: All archpriests and wealthy priests, as well as those who are not wealthy, must send their children to the Academy. This can also be prescribed for urban people of the upper class and officials of the central administration, while for the gentry, it shall be according to the personal desire of His Tsarist Majesty.

15. Those students who attend shall be present at the Academy until the end of all the studies, and the rector shall not release them from school without the consent of the Spiritual College. But if the rector or the prefect or someone else should release a student secretly

for a bribe, severe punishment shall be prescribed for such a criminal.

16. Let it be known everywhere to all that, where there is a person who has been educated in the Academy and certified by the Academy, an uneducated person cannot antecede him for a position involving an ecclesiastical or civil dignity, with great punishment for those authorities who would do otherwise.

17. The memory and intelligence of a newly arrived student shall be tested; and if he appears to be very dull, he shall not be accepted into the Academy, for he will lose years, but not learn anything. Rather he will gain the impression of himself that he is wise; and there are no worse good-for-nothings than these. Lest anyone feign mental inaptitude, desiring to be released home, as others feign physical disability to avoid military service, he shall be put to a testing of the mind for an entire year. An intelligent teacher can devise such methods of testing that the student will not be able to detect and circumvent them.

18. Should a youth appear to be intractably wicked, fierce, quick to fight, a scandalmonger, disobedient, and should it be impossible in a year's time to subdue him either by admonishments or severe punishments, he shall be expelled from the Academy even though he be intelligent, so as not to give a sword to a madman.

19. The location for the Academy is not to be in a city, but aside, in a suitably genial place, where there is no noise from people and where there are no frequent disturbances such as commonly hinder studies, create distractions in the minds of young people, and interfere with their efforts to persevere in learning.

20. The Academy should not boast or take the least notice that it has many students, for this is most vain. Rather it should consider how many there are who are intelligent and studying well, with promise of great benefit, and how to keep them constant to the end.

21. It is completely unnecessary, besides being useless, to accept whatever students may arrive for the sake of His Majesty's daily allowance of money. For many, some even by nature incapable, will come not for the sake of learning, but only for the salary, driven by abject need. Others, however, who are capable, will live at the Academy only as long as they desire, and then leave whenever and wherever they wish. What good is there from that? Only a futile loss.

Students should be accepted after an examination of their intelligence, and they should submit a written pledge that they shall remain at the Academy until the completion of their courses, subject to heavy punishment if they should not fulfill their promise, except out of extreme need. And thus it will be possible to present them, upon completion of school, to His Tsarist Majesty, and to appoint them in accordance with His Majesty's ukase to various assignments.

22. But what is most of all, and may be alone, necessary and beneficial is that there be a Seminary, similar to the many that have been created in foreign countries, attached to the Academy, or in the beginning even without the Academy, for the instruction and education of children. Herewith is presented a form for it:

(1) The building shall be constructed in the form of a monastery, whose extent and living quarters and all manner of supplies for subsistence and clothing and other requirements shall be over against the number of children (which shall be determined according to His Tsarist Majesty's desire): fifty or seventy or more, with the necessary administrators and servitors.

(2) In that building shall live children and youths of an already greater age, with eight or nine persons in a single dormitory, but with this arrangement: the oldest in a single dormitory, the middle in another, and the youngest in a third.

(3) Everyone shall be assigned a place beside the wall, instead of a personal room, where shall stand his cot (one that folds, lest it look during the day like a sleeping room), a chest for books and other things, and a small stool for sitting.

(4) In every dormitory (however many there may be), there shall be a prefect, or supervisor, a person of from thirty to fifty years of age who, even if unlearned, has nevertheless led an honorable life, only that he not be exceedingly harsh or a melancholic. His assignment is this: to supervise that among the seminarians (thus are called those being educated in that building) there be no quarrels, fights, coarse language, or any other disorder, and that at the set hours everyone does what he should. No seminarian shall leave his dormitory without his permission, and then with notification of the reason, where and for what he is leaving.

(5) In that building, it is fitting that there be at least three learned persons, monks or laymen, of whom one shall be the rector, the director of the entire building, and two examiners, that is,

inspectors of study, to see how one studies, slothfully or diligently.

(6) In each dormitory, the prefect shall have the authority to punish for an offense those subordinate to him, the youngest boys with the rod, the middle and oldest with a verbal warning, later reporting those who are incorrigible to the rector.

(7) Likewise shall the examiners deal with the youngest, middle, and oldest boys for laziness in study, and report to the rector.

(8) The rector, the highest authority of all, can punish with any punishment, according to the finding. The rector shall not release from the Seminary anyone who appears to be unyielding to correction without the consent of the Spiritual College.

(9) Times shall be assigned to the seminarians for every activity and relaxation, when to go to sleep, when to get up, to pray, to study, to go to the refectory, to stroll, etc. Each of those hours shall be designated by a bell, and all the seminarians, like soldiers upon a drumbeat, shall enter upon their work, whatever is scheduled for the set hour, upon the sound of bells.

(10) No seminarian shall be given leave from the Seminary into the cities, or anywhere else, to visit his family until he has become accustomed to live in the Seminary and has realized the obvious advantage of such an education; and namely: for three years after the arrival of anyone in the Seminary, he shall not be let out anywhere. Even after the third year he shall not be allowed to visit his parents or kinsmen more often than twice a year, and then not at a far distance, so that no more than seven days elapse from his departure until his return to the same Seminary building.

(11) When a seminarian is thus let out to visit, then he shall nevertheless be escorted by an honest person, such as an inspector, or supervisor, who shall accompany him everywhere and always and in all circumstances; and upon returning, he shall render a report to the rector on what occurred. But if that accompanying inspector, conniving with the seminarian, should conceal something bad, such a rogue shall be beaten severely. And that can be detected by the following, that the seminarian who has returned is unable not to show in himself a regression to his former ways and a loss of zeal.

(12) Whenever any kinsmen come to the Seminary to visit their kinsman there, those guests, with the rector's permission, shall be conducted into the refectory, or into some other common room, or

into the garden, and there they shall talk with their kinsman. They can be treated in moderation to food and drink, with the rector himself, or one of the examiners, being present, in keeping with their estimation of the guests.

(13) Such a way of life for young people appears to be irksome and similar to imprisonment. But for him who becomes accustomed to live thus, if even for a single year, it will be most agreeable.[78]

Nevertheless, for alleviating tedium, the following regulations are applicable:

(14) Only small children, from ten to fifteen years of age, shall be accepted in the Seminary, and older than that, only upon the petition of honest persons who bear witness that the lad lived in his parental home in fear and under good supervision.

(15) Every day two hours shall be assigned to the seminarians for recreation: namely, after dinner and after supper; and then, compulsorily, no one is to study or even have books in hand. The recreation should be by way of straightforward and physically active games: in the garden during summer and in their dormitory during winter. For this is beneficial to health and drives away monotony. And it is better yet to choose those games which, with amusement, afford some instruction: for example, sailing on water in real vessels, making geometrical measurements, constructing regular forts, etc.

(16) It is possible once or twice a month, especially in the summer, to travel to the islands, to the fields and places of enjoyment, to the Sovereign's country estates, and at least once a year, to Saint Petersburg.

(17) In the refectory, the reading shall be sometimes from military histories, sometimes from church histories. For two or three days at the beginning of each month, there shall be read the biographies of men who were brilliant in studies, of great Church teachers, and likewise, of ancient and contemporary philosophers, astronomers, rhetoricians, historians, etc. For the hearing of such biographies is agreeable and leads to imitation of those wise people.

(18) It is also possible twice a year or more to stage some performances, debates, comedies, and rhetorical exercises. For that not only is exceedingly beneficial for instruction and motivation, that is, toward the honest courage that preaching the word of God and diplomatic work [79] require, but such performances also make lively intermingling.

(19) Certain honors can be instituted for those who study well and carefully.

(20) On great holydays it is well that, at the table of those seminarians, there be the sound of musical instruments. And this is not difficult, for only one musician in the beginning need be hired. Those interested seminarians who have learned from him shall be obliged also to teach the others without charge. These seven aforementioned regulations are devoted to the entertainment of the students.

(21) It is fitting that there be in the Seminary a church, an apothecary, and a doctor, and for the classes to be in the nearby Academy, where the seminarians will go to learn. But if there are to be both classes and teachers in the Seminary, then the Academy and the Seminary shall be together. For the other students who might not desire to live in the Seminary, it is possible to construct several dwellings outside the Seminary and to put them up for rent to the students.

(22) The regulations that have been set forth above for the Academy in regard to teachers, to studies, and to students shall be observed here also.

(23) Only those seminarians who are indigent shall, through His Tsarist Majesty's bounty, receive subsistence, clothing, and other necessaries. But the other children of wealthy people shall be obliged to pay for food and clothing, and the price shall be uniform and determined once and for all.

(24) When a seminarian attains developed reason and progresses to higher studies, then he must take an oath in the Seminary church in the presence of the rest of his brethren that he desires to be faithful to His Tsarist Majesty and to his Heir, and that he is ready for the service to which he is suited and to which he shall be summoned by the Sovereign's ukase.

(25) The rector shall not release from the Seminary those seminarians who have completed their studies until he has first notified the Spiritual College and the College shall have presented them to His Tsarist Majesty. Then they shall be given a discharge, together with an attestation of their proficiency.

(26) Those seminarians who, after the completion of studies, appear to be the most suited for ecclesiastical work should be, in the consideration of bishops, nearer to all the positions of authority than

others who may be as equally proficient as they, unless some obvious vice that is not imputed through slander is evident in the seminarian. Severe punishment shall be prescribed for those who envy and slander.

The preceding provisions have concerned the Seminary.

It will be possible in the future to formulate additional plans or to search out ideas from the best foreign seminaries. From such education and instruction, great usefulness to the fatherland can truly be expected.

23. *As to Preachers of God's Word, the Following Regulations Are Applicable.*

(1) No one shall venture to preach who has not been taught in this Academy and who is not certified by the Academy. But if someone has studied among people of another faith, he should present himself before the Spiritual College, and there he shall be tested on how versed he is in Holy Scripture. Also he shall deliver a sermon on a topic that the College shall prescribe. If he appears to be proficient, then he shall be given an attestation that, if he should wish to become a priest, he may preach.

(2) Preachers should preach firmly, with argument from Holy Scripture, on repentance, on regeneration of life, on respect for the authorities, especially the supreme authority of the Tsar, and on the obligations of every class. They should extirpate superstition; they should implant in people's hearts the fear of God. In a word, they should ascertain from Holy Scripture that the will of God is holy, beneficent, and perfect, and they should declare it.

(3) They shall speak on the sins in society, but they shall not name anyone unless it is announced through the whole Church.

But when some malicious rumor is spread in regard to a certain person concerning this or that particular sin, then a preacher is obliged to keep silent in the sermon about such a sin. For if he should mention that sin, even though he does not mention the person specifically, the people nevertheless will surmise that he is the person against whom the thunder is directed. His distress thus will increase and he will begin to think not of his own regeneration, but rather, about vengeance against that preacher. What is the use of that? If someone's sin is grievous, involving contempt for God's Law, it will of its own accord become manifest in an arrogant sinner. Then it is for a bishop, and not some presbyter, to impose a penalty upon him by such means as were described above with reference to bishops' cases concerning anathema.

(4) If anyone has angered them in something, it is the habit of some preachers to take vengeance against him in their sermon. While not by name tearing his reputation to pieces, yet they speak in such a way that it is possible for the congregation to know who is being spoken about. Such preachers are the worst good-for-nothings, and they should be made subject to severe punishment.

(5) It is exceedingly unbecoming for a preacher, especially a young one, to speak about the sins of the authorities or reproachfully in the face of the congregation. Thus, for example: "You have no fear of God; you have no love for your neighbor; you are merciless; you wrong one another." But he must speak thus, in the first person, plural number: "We have no fear of God; we do not have love for our neighbor; we are merciless; we wrong one another." For this is a humble form, since the preacher includes himself in the ranks of the sinners, as it is indeed true, for we all sin greatly. Thus, reproaching the teachers who, regarding themselves highly, desired to be known to their disciples by their own names, Apostle Paul, not mentioning them specifically, takes that blame upon himself, as it were, and also upon his friends, Peter and Apollos, in the First Epistle to the Corinthians, the first chapter.[80] "Each of you," he declares, "says, I am of Paul, or I am of Cephas, or I am of Christ. Has Christ been divided up? Was Paul crucified for you? Or were you baptized in the name of Paul?" etc. That he transferred this blame to himself and to others he himself attests. For, after having spoken at length about that, he confesses in the fourth chapter: [81] "These things, my brothers, I have applied to myself and Apollos for your [82] sake, so that you may learn not to speculate more than what is written," etc.

(6) Every preacher must have at hand the books of Saint John Chrysostom and read them diligently, as in this way he will become accustomed to putting together a most articulate and clear sermon, even if it is not equal to Chrysostom's. But he should not read light-minded sermonizers, such as abound especially among the Poles.

(7) If a preacher sees the people benefit from his sermon, then let him not boast about it. If he does not see any benefit, let him not be angry and inveigh against the people because of this. Their task is to speak, but the turning of human hearts is the task of God. "I have planted, Apollos watered, but God has given the growth." [83]

(8) Foolishly do those preachers behave who raise their eyebrows, display haughty movement of the shoulders, and prattle such things in a sermon that it is evident they are amazed at themselves. But a prudent teacher will, as much as possible, strive to show, both by his speech and the action of the entire body, that he does not even think about his astuteness or eloquence. Accordingly it is fitting often to combine brief admonitions with a certain humbling of oneself. For example: "I beseech your love, that you do not take notice who is speaking; for what testimony can I give about myself, except that I am a sinner?" "Believe the word of God, for I endeavor to expound from Holy Scriptures and not my imagination," and others similar to these.

(9 A preacher should not rock back and forth excessively as though he were rowing a boat with an oar. He should not clasp his hands, put them on his hips, jump up and down, laugh or weep; but even if his spirit be troubled, he should, as much as possible, repress his tears. For all these are superfluous and undecorous, and perturb the congregation.

(10) After the sermon, if he happens to be on a visit or engaged in conversation, it is not fitting for a preacher to reminisce about his sermon. Not only should he refrain from praising his own sermon, which is egregious effrontery, but likewise deliberately from disparaging it, for it will appear that in this way he prompts others in the praise of his sermon. Even if someone should begin to praise his sermon, a preacher must show that he is embarrassed to hear it and by all possible means steer from the compliments and start a different conversation.

Laymen, Insofar as They Are Concerned with Religious Instruction

Although it is not necessary to say much in this brief section, it is nevertheless fitting to set forth a small introduction for a better understanding of why laymen are called such and how they differ from the clergy.

The term "world" is used in a threefold sense:

1. Everything under the sun inhabited by people is called the world. But it is not in this sense that persons without a religious vocation are called worldly people, or laymen, for priests live in the same world with everybody else.

2. "World" is taken to mean simply people, as physical but rational creatures. And it is not as regards this world that we call laymen those who are distinct from persons who serve the Church. For no priest or any other churchman would wish to refuse to be called a worldly person in this sense. In this same sense, the term "world" is applied where something good is attributed to it, for example: "God so loved the world," [84] etc.

3. "World" often signifies human wickedness and vanity, or the people themselves insofar as they are wicked and vain, as Apostle John says in his First Epistle, the second chapter: "Do not love the world, or the things that are in the world. If anyone loves the world, the love of the Father is not in him; because all that is in the world is the lust of the flesh, and the lust of the eyes, and the pride of life; which is not from the Father, but from the world." [85] And it is not from this world that laymen are so called, for John is not writing to the priesthood, but to Christians generally. And since he himself in that same place [86] speaks to fathers, youths, and children, that is, to all of every age, it cannot be said that he through this writing is urging them to become monks or ecclesiastics.

Similarly the word "spiritual," or "clerical," which is the opposite of "worldly," or "laic," as used in this third sense, does not refer to monks themselves or to ecclesiastics in Apostle Paul's First Epistle to the Corinthians, at the end of the second chapter,[87] where he discusses the sensual and the spiritual man. For he calls him sensual who, by himself, without the blessing of the Holy Ghost, is inclined to every evil and is powerless as regards what is good and pleasing in the sight of God, as are all who are not renewed. He calls a spiritual man him who has been enlightened and renewed, and who is guided by the Holy Ghost. If, then, a priest is more like an evil layman, he is a sensual man; if, conversely, a priest is like a layman who is guided by the Holy Ghost, he is a spiritual man. That is why Saint Peter ascribes the name "priesthood" not to church ministers alone, but generally to all Christians (1 Pet. 2).[88] "You, however, are a chosen race, a royal priesthood, a holy nation, a purchased people; that you may proclaim the perfections of him who has called you out of darkness into his marvellous light." Likewise, the Apocalypse, chapter 5: [89] ". . . and hast made them for our God a kingdom and priests."

It was fitting to explain this because, through ignorance of it, much spiritually baneful nonsense is done and said. A lay person, not realizing this, sometimes thinks that he cannot be saved precisely because he is not spiritual but worldly. Not realizing this, some monk will urge a man to leave wife, children, and parents, and to despise them; for, says he, "We have a commandment: 'Do not love the world and those who are in the world.'"

But why are laymen so called? Answer. It was fitting that there be appointed ministers and directors of spiritual instruction, such as are the bishops and presbyters. Accordingly, for the sake of a certain distinction, they assumed titles of ecclesiastical office. And because they offer bloodless sacrifices, they are distinguished by being called priests. Therefore the others, who are their congregation and disciples, are called simply laymen.

You say: "Therefore, in accordance with which of the three meanings for 'world' mentioned above are worldly people, or laymen, so called?"

This name appertains to the second meaning, for all, both priests and nonpriests, are worldly people, that is, human beings. But nonpriests are called laymen only insofar as they are not appointed directors and ministers of religious instruction, but are the congregation. Now it is necessary to say something about laymen insofar as they are submitted to spiritual administration.

1. Let this first be known to all, that every Christian must hear Orthodox instruction from his pastors. For as pastors do not tend their flocks if they do not nourish their sheep with God's word, likewise the sheep are not sheep, but are called so in vain, if they do not wish to be taken care of by the pastor. Wherefore, if someone should disdain or abuse, or worse, if he should strive to prevent, the reading or preaching of God's word only through a certain haughty wickedness and without extreme necessity, he shall be subject to ecclesiastical punishment, either to the judgment of the bishop, about which there was a statement made above in reference to anathema, or if he shows resistance, by the investigation and decree of the Spiritual College itself.

2. Every Christian is obliged to receive Holy Communion often, at least once a year. For this is our finest thanksgiving to God for the glorious salvation wrought for us by the Savior's death ("For as

often as you shall eat this bread and drink the cup, you proclaim the death of the Lord, until he comes" [90]) and the viaticum for eternal life ("Unless you eat the flesh of the Son of Man, and drink his blood, you shall not have life in you" [91]). It is a mark, or sign, by which we show ourselves to be members of the single Mystical Body of Christ, that is, fellow-members of the one Holy Church, as the Apostle says in 1 Corinthians, chapter 10.[92] "The cup of blessing that we bless, is it not the sharing of the blood of Christ? And the bread that we break, is it not the partaking of the body of the Lord? Because the bread is one, we though many, are one body, all of us who partake of the one bread." Accordingly, if some Christian appears to stay away from Holy Communion a great deal, he thereby reveals himself to be not in the Body of Christ, that is, he is not a fellow-member of the Church, but is a schismatic. And there is no better sign that allows to recognize a schismatic. Bishops should diligently watch for this, and order that parish priests, year after year, report their parishioners, who among them did not receive Communion during the year, who did not do so for two years, and who never has received Communion. Such persons are to be required to render a sworn confession as to whether they are sons of the Church and whether they condemn all the hosts of schismatics who are to be found throughout Russia. That demand for an oath is to be nothing other than a warning that, if they should not wish to swear and condemn specifically all the schismatic sects, an announcement shall be issued about them, that they are schismatics. It is of not little benefit to know about this, for many schismatics, hiding under the appearance of Orthodoxy, instead of being afraid, do themselves raise up a persecution against the Church. Not only do they abuse the priesthood and harm it as much as they can, but by all possible means they oppress laymen who do not agree with their lunacy, to which trustworthy people can bear witness.

3. When a schismatic is proclaimed in this or some other manner, then a bishop must forward information in writing concerning that schismatic to whoever exercises legal jurisdiction over him, and he, in turn, shall send him to the Spiritual College.

4. It is useful to have in the College information on how many schismatics are to be found in all the eparchies, for this is helpful in many cases that require a determination.

5. It is a grievous sin, which does not permit silence on the part

of ecclesiastics, that some laic lords who are aware of schismatics in their regions shield them for the bribe offered to them.

It is another matter in regard to known schismatics, for it is not necessary to guard against their attack. But to shield schismatics who live under the appearance of Orthodoxy is a matter that smells of godlessness. Bishops must be zealous in this and report it to the Spiritual College; and the College, after a spiritual investigation, may anathematize such lords if they should not desire to amend themselves in that.[93] It is fitting that the spiritual investigation take this form: A bishop shall not simply submit a report to the Spiritual College against a laic lord that schismatics are to be found in his domains, but that the lord forcibly does not allow his parish priest, or one sent by the bishop, to search out and expose the schismatics who dwell on his estate. And named in that report shall be reliable witnesses thereto. The College, having heard the witnesses, shall write exhortatively to that lord that he permit a search for schismatics to be freely conducted on his estate. If the lord obeys, then he is not to be troubled further; if he disobeys, then he himself, by his action, bears witness regarding himself that he is a defender of schismatics. Whereupon the College shall proceed to his spiritual punishment in strict adherence to the established procedure described above in reference to anathema. This is a matter, as declared above, that concerns not known but clandestine schismatics provided that they are ordinary persons; but if they are schismatic teachers and so-called pastors, then this matter concerns them whether they be known or clandestine. In this same manner shall be judged ecclesiastics who have their own followers.

6. Throughout all Russia, no schismatic shall be elevated to a position of not only spiritual, but also civil authority, even to the least important position of supervision and administration, lest we arm against ourselves ferocious enemies who incessantly ponder evil for the state and for the Sovereign.

Anyone suspected of being a schismatic even if he has the appearance of Orthodoxy, shall first of all be sworn in, together with an oath as regards himself in relation to schismatics, that he is not and does not intend to be a schismatic; he shall be informed of severe punishment if afterwards he shows evidence of anything to the contrary; and he shall sign this with his own hand. And his guilt is shown by some overt action on his part which places him under suspicion: for example,* [94] if he abstains from receiving the Holy Mysteries without legitimate cause; if there are schismatic teachers in his house and he shelters them knowing that they are such; if he sends alms to schismatic cloisters, etc. If anyone is exposed in such activities upon clear evidence, then he shall be liable to suspicion of schism.

If anything contrary to this appears, then a bishop must expeditiously write about it to the Spiritual College.

7. Henceforth no laymen whosoever (except His Tsarist Majesty's family) shall have in their homes private churches or priests whom they nominate themselves, for this is unnecessary.[95] It is done only through pride and draws reproach upon the clergy. The lords should go to the parish churches and should not be ashamed to be brothers even with their own peasants in the Christian community. Says the Apostle, "For in Christ Jesus, there is neither slave nor freeman." [96]

8. When parishioners or landlords who live on their own estates select a person to be the priest of their church, then they must give testimony in their report that he is a person of good background and free of suspicion. In the case of landlords who do not themselves live on their estates, their people and peasants shall submit that testimony concerning such persons, and they shall write in their petitions exactly how much prestimony or land he is to receive. And he who is selected shall likewise add a written statement that he is willing to be satisfied with that prestimony or land, and that he shall not leave the church to which he is consecrated until death. But if he who is selected appears to the bishop as being somehow suspect, or in schism and unworthy of that rank, this shall be left to the bishop's determination.

9. The lords should not accept vagrant priests as their confessors. For a priest who has been banished because of a crime, or who of his own volition has abandoned a church entrusted to him, is already almost not a priest, and he commits a grievous sin by exercising the priestly function. The lord who accepts him is an accomplice in that sin, and doubly so, for he is an abettor of that sin and a foe of ecclesiastical administration.

Powerful laymen should not require priests to enter their homes

* A printed ukase of Our Great Sovereign concerning this was promulgated in 1718.

for baptizing children, but should carry them to church unless the infant is extremely ill or some other serious emergency intervenes.

10. It is reported that civil administrators or other authorities, as well as willful landlords, sometimes do not desire to obey the bishops in whose eparchy they live in some matter that has arisen and calls for religious instruction, pleading that the bishop is not their pastor. Let it be known to all that every person, of whatever rank, is subject in spiritual matters to the judgment of that bishop in whose eparchy he resides, for as long as he resides there.

11. Many difficulties especially befall laymen in questionable marriages, and for that reason, if such a question does befall someone, he should not venture to conceal it from the priest. And the priest, if he himself is uncertain, shall not venture to solemnize the marriage hastily, but shall refer the matter to the bishop's determination. But even the bishop should forward it to the Spiritual College if he is unable himself to decide.

And for a proper and incontestable resolution of such difficulties, it is incumbent upon the members of the Spiritual College, having selected a particular time, to discuss them adequately and, for every difficulty, to write a definitive decision from Holy Scripture and from the decisions of the ancient glorious teachers, as well as from the Tsar's regulations.

12. And although someone's marriage should be deemed to be unobjectionable, it is nevertheless not fitting to be wed in another parish, in which neither the groom nor the bride resides; moreover, it is not fitting to be wed in another episcopate. Likewise priests shall not be called from a different parish or eparchy for nuptials, for this, besides being a reproach to their own pastors, also indicates that those who are thus married are under suspicion of an irregular union.

PART III. THE RESPONSIBILITY, FUNCTION,
AND POWER OF THE ADMINISTRATORS THEMSELVES,
OF WHOM THE SPIRITUAL COLLEGE IS COMPOSED

1. Twelve is a suitable number of administrators. They are to be persons of different ranks: bishops, archimandrites, hegumens, archpriests. Of this number, three shall be bishops, while the rest shall come from whoever is found to be worthy in the other ranks.

2. It is to be observed that in the membership of this assembly

there shall not be archimandrites or archpriests who are the subordinates of some bishop in this assembly, for such an archimandrite or archpriest will be constantly watching: whichever side being judged the bishop favors, that side will the archimandrite and archpriest favor. Thus two or three individuals will be as one person. Further it is fitting to examine what the Spiritual College ought to do, how it should function and act in matters that have been submitted, and what power it possesses for the settlement of cases. And these three appear as the three things named above in the title of this part, for they are the responsibility, the function, and the power. Something special shall be said about each.

Responsibility

1. The first, and almost the only, responsibility of this Spiritual College is to be aware of what are the obligations both of all Christians generally and particularly of bishops, presbyters, together with other church servitors, monks, teachers, and students, and also of laymen, insofar as they are concerned with religious instruction. Accordingly there are recorded herein some of the obligations of all those ranks. And the Spiritual College must watch whether each remains in his calling, and instruct and punish those who err. But here are incorporated specifically some of the responsibilities of this administration.

2. It shall notify or announce to all Christians generally, of whatever rank, that anyone who has noticed something that may be useful for the improved administration of the Church may report it in a letter to the Spiritual College, just as anyone may freely report to the Senate concerning regular profits for the state. The Spiritual College shall decide whether the advice is useful or useless; and it shall adopt the useful, while the useless shall be rejected.

3. If someone writes a theological work on some subject, then it should not be printed until after it has first been submitted to the College. And the College must examine it to see whether there is some error in that work that is contrary to Orthodox teaching.

4. If an incorruptible body appears somewhere, or if rumors arise about an apparition or a miracle, the College must ascertain the truth of it, having summoned to an inquiry those informants and others who are able to give testimony about it.

5. If someone denounces a person as schismatic or as an innovator of some new teaching, that shall be judged in the Spiritual College.

6. There occur certain perplexing moral predicaments, as for example, what to do when someone who has stolen another's property wishes to return it but cannot either through shame or fear, or because the other person, from whom he stole, has passed away. And what is he to do who chanced to be among pagans involuntarily, accepted their godless faith to gain his freedom, and later returns to the Christian confession? These and other problems shall be brought to the Spiritual College, which shall diligently deliberate and decide them.

7. Those who are to be elevated to the episcopate shall here first be examined as to whether they are superstitious persons, bigots, or simoniacs, and where and how they have lived. An examination, with testimony, shall be made of the source of a candidate's wealth, if such a person appears.

8. If anyone is not satisfied with them, the judgments of bishops shall be referred to the judgment of the Spiritual College. These matters are subject to judgment: namely, doubtful marriages, unlawful divorces, injuries to the clergy or to a monastery brought about by their bishop, or injuries caused to a bishop by another bishop. In brief, all those matters that were subject to the judgment of the Patriarch.

9. The College must examine who exercises control over church lands, and how; and where and for what the grain and profits, if there are any monetary ones, are expended. If someone surreptitiously steals church chattels, the Spiritual College shall bear down on him and must recover from him what was stolen.

10. When a bishop, or some lesser servant of the Church, suffers an injury from some powerful lord, even if it is necessary to seek justice against him not in the Spiritual College, but in the Judicial College, or subsequently, in the Senate, the injured party shall nevertheless disclose his exigency to the Spiritual College also. And then the president and all the College, extending assistance to their injured brother, shall dispatch honest men in their name to petition for expeditious justice, wherever it is fitting.

11. If the last wills or testaments of distinguished personages

should appear to be questionable in some respect, they shall be reported to the Spiritual College and to the Judicial College, and both these Colleges shall deliberate and lay down a decision.

12. The Spiritual College must compose an instruction concerning almsgiving, for in this we do err not a little. Many sluggards in perfect health set out in their laziness begging for alms and they wander shamelessly about the land; others install themselves under false pretenses in the poorhouses of the elders, which is odious to God and harmful to the fatherland. God commands us to eat bread by the sweat of our brow, that is, by righteous works and diverse labors (Gen. 3),[97]; and to do good not only for personal gain, but that we yet may have something to give to those in need, that is, to the poor (Eph. 5) [98]; and God forbids that an idle person even eat (2 Thess. 3).[99] Accordingly, healthy but lazy beggars are repugnant to God. If anyone provisions them, he is as an accomplice in it and likewise a participant in their sin; and whatever he expends on such vain almsgiving, instead of being to his spiritual benefit, gains for him no merit. But from such preposterous almsgiving there is caused, as we said, great harm to the fatherland, for from this, first of all, shortages develop and grain becomes expensive. Let any reasonable person consider how many thousands of such lazy beggars are to be found in Russia; those thousands do not produce grain, and accordingly, there is no grain yield from them. Nevertheless, with impudence and cunning humility, they eat the labors of others. Therefore much consumption of grain is of no use. Such persons should be seized everywhere and consigned to public works. For, on account of those beggars, great injury is done to those who are really poor; as much as is given to them, so much is taken away from the genuinely poor. And those sluggards, since they are healthy, come running quickly to the alms, while the feeble poor are left behind. Some lie almost half dead in the streets, withering away in their sickness and starvation. Such persons are they that, having been deprived of daily food, they are ashamed to ask. If someone has the genuine spirit of charity, he cannot but desire from his heart, having considered these things, that there be suitable correction of such disorder.

On top of that, those indolent rogues compose certain insane and spiritually harmful songs, and sing them before the people with sham groaning. Then, accepting remuneration for it, they madden yet more the simple oafs.

And who can briefly calculate the damage being perpetrated by such good-for-nothings? Along the roads, wherever they look, they ravage. They are incendiaries. They are engaged for spying by rebels and traitors. They asperse high authorities and wickedly malign the supreme authority itself. They incline the common people to contempt for the authorities. They do not concern themselves with any Christian duties. They fancy that to attend church is not their affair, but that they are only to wail incessantly before some church. And this exceeds even the limit of their depravity and inhumanity: they blind the eyes of their own children, they warp their arms, and they deform their other members, so that they will be genuine paupers and deserving of charity. Truly there exists no more lawless class of people. Thus there is incumbent upon the Spiritual College the great obligation to think about this diligently, to advise by what means it would be best to eradicate this evil, and to determine a good system for almsgiving, and having decided upon it to request His Tsarist Majesty that he allow it to be sanctioned by his own monarchal ukase.

13. And this is not a trifling obligation: how to turn the priesthood away from simony and shameless impudence. For this, it is useful to assemble in council with the senators to determine the number of households for one parish, from which everyone shall pay a specified tax to the priesthood and other churchmen of his church, so that, as far as possible, they will have complete self-sufficiency and will not henceforth solicit payment for baptism, burial, marriage, etc.

However, this decision shall not prohibit benevolent persons from donating to a priest as much as they desire according to their generosity.

Each member of the College, even as the president, so also the rest, at the commencement of his assumption of office, must take an oath that he is and shall be faithful to His Tsarist Majesty; that he shall consider matters and render advice not according to his passions and not for recompense, but for the sake of God and the people's weal, with the fear of God and a good conscience, and in the same way he shall deliberate the opinions and recommendations of his other confreres, whether they are to be accepted or rejected. And he shall bind himself by this oath under explicit penalty of anathema and corporal punishment if afterwards he is discovered and disclosed to be in violation of his oath.

All this written herein His Most Holy Tsarist Majesty, the All-Russian Monarch himself first vouchsafed, in the year 1720, the eleventh day of February, to hear read before him and to deliberate and amend it. And later, by the ukase of His Majesty, the Holy Bishops and Archimandrites, jointly with the Ruling Senators, heard it, and having deliberated, amended it on the twenty-third day of February. Likewise, for its sanction and immutable execution, following the affixture of signatures by the ecclesiastical and senatorial persons attending, His Tsarist Majesty himself consented to sign it with his own hand.[100]

Supplement to the Spiritual Regulation

ON THE RULES FOR PARISH CLERGY
AND THE MONASTIC LIFE [101]

ALTHOUGH in the matters pertaining to bishops discussed here-inbefore certain rules are to be found that serve for the improvement of the priesthood, as well as monastic life, yet because those are insufficient the Most Holy Ruling Synod [102] is obliged, by the personal ukase of His Imperial Majesty, printed at the beginning of the *Regulation,* to supplement in future time its *Regulation* with new rules. Accordingly, by the force of that ukase, there are incorporated herein specific rules serving for the improvement of parish churchmen, as well as of monastic life, with the approval of His Imperial Majesty and with the concurrence of the Most Holy Ruling Synod, and ratified by the signatures of all the members of the Synod.

ON PRESBYTERS, DEACONS, AND OTHER CHURCHMEN

Sufficiently well did God impart instructions to priests and deacons through Apostle Paul: Acts, chapter 20; [103] 1 Timothy, chapter 3; [104] Titus, chapter 1.[105] If they had kept what was commanded by him, there would not have been required more ecclesiastical canons and rules. But whereas, in time, the parish clergy appeared to be not a little corrupt, accordingly the holy fathers, at different councils, issued many canons for their regeneration in accordance with the manifest needs of the times. There is no need to incorporate herein all those canons, which are contained in the books of the councils. Because particular weaknesses are to be seen in the parish clergy of our Russian Church, for that reason it is fitting to devise specific improvements, in addition to the previous ones, in accordance with God's word, after the example of the ancient fathers, so that bishops shall then understand what they must watch for in their churchmen and the churchmen shall know the true path of their calling, and so that this grand administration, the Most Holy Synod, shall be better able to function in the general supervision of the ecclesiastical estate.

1. Many do insinuate themselves into the priesthood for no other reason than only for greater freedom and subsistence, and they do not possess any requisite aptitude for their vocation. Accordingly no one shall be installed as a priest or deacon who has not been instructed in a bishop's household school (about which there was a statement in reference to espicopal matters in Article 10). And until those schools come into being, candidates shall be directed to study books on the faith and Christian law; and a candidate shall not be installed until he has committed them to memory.

2. An arriving candidate shall have, in a deposition, authentic testimony from his parishioners that they know him to be a good person: namely, not a drunkard, not an idler in the maintenance of his household, not a scandalmonger, not a querulous grumbler, not a fornicator, not a brawler, and not accused demonstrably in deception and fraud. For these misdeeds in particular impede the work of a pastor and lend to the clergy a wretched aspect.

3. In that same deposition, there shall be specifically indicated, under the signatures of the parishioners, the prestimony or land allocated to the priest of that parish, and under the signature of the candidate, that he is willing to be satisfied with that prestimony or land.

4. An accepted candidate shall not be immediately installed, but he should first master the books referred to. Meanwhile he shall be tested as to whether he is a bigot and feigns humility, which for an intelligent person it is not difficult to find out. Likewise whether he speaks of his dreams and apparitions concerning himself or anyone else. For what good can be hoped for from such persons except old wives' tales and harmful vagaries among the people instead of salutary teaching?

5. Before his installation into the priesthood, a candidate shall in church publicly condemn specifically all schismatic sects, together with an oath that he shall not shelter by silence whomever he finds in the parish, through their estrangement from the Holy Eucharist or through other signs, to be clandestine schismatics, but shall render a report in writing concerning them to his bishop.[106] Along with the aforementioned oath, he must take an oath of loyalty to his Sovereign, and inform of all opposition, as well as whatever matters he is by the rules ordered to report, which someone may mention even during confession, but of which he does not repent and with respect to which he does not lay aside his intention, as is clearly indicated hereunder in Article 11.

6. Until a candidate's installation into the priesthood, while he is learning the church services in a bishop's house, let him copy for himself these rules for priests inscribed herein if he is unable to have a printed *Regulation;* likewise, the aforestated rules on general matters from the *Regulation;* and third, the aforestated rules for laymen, so that in the future he shall not excuse himself through ignorance of his obligations. And prior to his release, let there be recorded an acknowledgment in the episcopal chancery that he took with him the rules referred to and that he shall acquit himself in compliance with them, subject to punishment according to the judgment of the bishop. At the time that the bishop visits his eparchy, he must show these rules to the bishop.

7. Priests must especially know these things: in confession, if they encounter someone who is cold and without emotion, how to terrify with God's judgment him who is confessing; if they see someone who is skeptical and inclined to despair, how to restore such a one, and how to strengthen him with the hope of God's mercy and kindness; how to instruct one in the breaking of a sinful habit; how to visit and comfort a sick person; how to sustain and administer to the passing of a dying person with words; and how, especially, to support those who have been sentenced and are being led to death, and reassure them of God's mercy. These are truly the most necessary duties of priests.

But since these cannot be expected from a priesthood that is little educated, for that reason (until God grants to see in Russia complete education), it is fitting to write out the parts serving the aforementioned needs. Then a priest, after having committed them to memory, should either say them or read them to a sick person, a dying person, to one being led to death, and in rendering all his other ministration.

8. To those who come to him for confession, a priest shall not be oppressive. He becomes oppressive when, either at the time of confession, he prides himself and appears stern to him who is confessing, whom he ought to comfort with all humility, or at other times, when he impudently asks for something from his spiritual sons, or as it were, importunes with authority. For example: to request or importune a person in authority that he acquit somone in a judicial action, or that he remit a punishment, even though that would be inequitable to the plaintiffs or detrimental to the people. If such arrogant good-for-nothings appear, the authority of the confessional shall be immediately banned to them.

9. And there is yet even a greater misdeed: if a priest reveals in a quarrel the sins of his spiritual son. For this he shall be divested of the priesthood, and he shall be referred to a lay tribunal for corporal punishment in accordance with the determination of the matter.

10. But every confessor must keep from quarreling with his spiritual children, for whatever he spews against them as being reprehensible, those who are present will think that he knows about it from confession, and thus, a slander will become credible and, for that reason, insufferable. For this, confessors who sin thus are liable to severe punishment.

11. If someone in confession informs his spiritual father of some illegality that has not been committed, but that he yet intends to commit, especially treason or mutiny against the Sovereign or against the state, or evil designs upon the honor or well-being of the Sovereign and upon His Majesty's family, and in informing of such a great intended evil, he reveals himself as not repenting but considers himself in the right, does not lay aside his intention, and does not confess it as though it were a sin, but rather, so that with his confessor's assent or silence he might become confirmed in his intention—what can be concluded therefrom is this: When the spiritual father, in God's name, enjoins him to abandon completely his evil intention, and he, silently, as though undecided or justifying himself, does not appear to have changed his mind, then the confessor must not only not honor as valid the forgiveness and remission of the confessed sins, for it is not a regular confession if someone

does not repent of all his transgressions, but he must expeditiously report concerning them, where it is fitting, pursuant to His Imperial Majesty's personal ukase, promulgated on the twenty-eighth day of April of the present year, 1722,[107] which was published in printed form with reference to these misdeeds, in accordance with which it is ordered to bring such malefactors to designated places, exercising the greatest speed, even as the result of statements concerning His Imperial Majesty's high honor and damaging to the state. Wherefore a confessor, in compliance with the provisions of that personal ukase of His Imperial Majesty, must immediately report, to whom it is appropriate, such a person who thus displays in confession his evil and unrepentant intention. However, in that report, the salient points of what has transpired in confession shall not be disclosed, since in accordance with that ukase, it is prohibited to interrogate such malefactors, who appear in connection with making the aforementioned damaging statements, anywhere except in the Privy Chancery or in the Preobrazhensky Central Administrative Office. But in that report shall only be stated secretly that such a person, indicating therein his name and rank, harbors evil ideas and impenitent intent against the Sovereign or against the rest of what was referred to above, from which he desires that there be great harm: Therefore he must be apprehended and placed under arrest without delay. And whereas, by that same personal ukase of His Imperial Majesty, it is ordered to send the informers also, under surety furnished by guarantors, or if there are no guarantors, under escort in honorable arrest, to the aforementioned Privy Chancery or the Preobrazhensky Central Administrative Office for proper arraignment of those malefactors, accordingly a priest who has reported that matter, after giving surety for himself, shall proceed, upon being dispatched, to the prescribed place without postponement or evasion. And there, where investigation is made into such misdeeds, he shall report specifically, without any concealment or indecision, everything that was heard regarding that evil intention. For, by this report, the confessor does not disclose a genuine confession and does not transgress the canons, but rather fulfills the Lord's teaching, spoken thus: "If thy brother sin against thee, go and show him his fault, between thee and him alone. If he listen to thee, thou hast won thy brother," [108] etc. "If he refuses to listen, tell it to the church." * [109]

* Matt. 18: 15, 16, 17.[110]

Wherefore it can be concluded that when the Lord commands to notify the Church even over a brother's sin in a matter involving only a single wrong, or in a matter touching on something similar to that, in which a person does not repent and remains disobedient, then how much more is it obligatory to report and inform about an evil design against the Sovereign or against the body of the Church and about the harm desired therefrom. With respect to that, every confessor should recall that at ordination a bishop personally enjoins in the following manner every priest in the charter of ordination given to him by the bishop in accordance with ancient patristic tradition: "With deliberation you shall bind and loose the sins of those confessing their sins according to the canons," etc.; and, "According to our episcopal blessing and command, the more serious and difficult offenses shall be brought to us." Since it was established in the past for a confessor thus to bring to a bishop the more serious and difficult offenses that had already been confessed with repentance, then how much more is it appropriate to inform concerning an impenitent intention and evil design against the Sovereign or against the state. By this notification, the confession is not impaired, since the declaration of an intended crime, which the person confessing does not desire to abandon and does not regard as a sin on his part, is not a confession, nor even part of a confession, but is an insidious contrivance for the seduction of his own conscience, leading to perdition for those malefactors and doom for their confessors who conceal such evil intention, which indeed was clearly demonstrated not only in years past, but even this year.[111] With respect to this, in the Most Holy Synod's own announcement to the spiritual and priestly rank, promulgated on the seventeenth day of May of the present year, 1722, specific explanations were provided for the benefit of those who are directed to take such measures and the propriety of such notification was adequately substantiated therein.[112]

12. Not only must priests inform of an evil that seeks to be put into action, but also of a scandal that has already been perpetrated against the people. For example: when someone, having imagined it somewhere in some way or having hypocritically contrived it, spreads the news of a false miracle and the ordinary, undiscriminating people accept it as real. Later, if such a fabricator discloses that to be a fantasy of his in confession, but does not display repentance for it and does not promise to make it known publicly (so that the

ignorant may not accept that lie as real), that lie, being accepted as real through ignorance, will be added to the number of genuine miracles and in time will for everyone become firmly established in memory and renown. Therefore a confessor must inform of that, where it is fitting, without delay, so that such a falsehood may be halted and the people, beguiled by that lie, might not sin through ignorance and accept that lie as real. For, by use of such false miracles, not only is contumely of one kind or another perpetrated, but God's commandment, "You shall not take the name of the Lord, your God, in vain," [113] is violated. Those who recount such miracles use God's name in a lie, so that it is not glorified by them, but is taken in vain. And upon the piety of Orthodox believers descends censure from those of other faiths. Accordingly it is most necessary to halt such illegal and impious activity; and confessors, as was mentioned herein, must inform of such cases without concealment and immediately.

13. Whenever something other than those most important causes for the submission of reports has been confessed with repentance and the intention of atonement, and yet it appears to a confessor as a sin difficult to resolve, that is, as a grievous sin that requires some correction and expiation, the confessor shall go to his bishop, and not naming the penitent, he must set forth the sin in detail and ask for a decision.

14. Many priests who are not proficient in letters cling to the missal [114] like blind men, forbidding Communion to penitents for many years. In doing so they profess what is written, but the purpose of it they do not know; and in such unreason they do not consider others to be worthy of Communion even at death. They excuse themselves by saying that the administration of Holy Communion is not permissible without penance. But death does not wait for him who is ill to do penance.[115] Accordingly the following argument is propounded.

The ancient holy fathers and pastors did not reason thus about penances, as though they were more difficult to change than dogmas. But they modified them, and they permitted them to be modified, having for that certain sound reasons, as the testimony of some of the holy fathers here shows. Basil the Great, in the third canon, says: "It is fitting for us to know both what is an immutable law and what is a custom. In matters not determined by immutable law, one should act in consonance with traditional custom." In this same discourse there is a statement by Basil on penances: He considers them as determined and imposed not in keeping with any immutable law, but in accordance with custom, whatever it may be in a given place. That same teacher reasons thus in canon 74 on penances: "If anyone who has become entangled with the sins that we mentioned above appears to be set fully aright through confession, then the spiritual father, having received from God's love of man the authority to bind and loose, will not be deserving of reproach if, seeing the pure repentance of the penitent, he shows kindness to him by shortening the period of penance." Of this work by Basil, Theodore Balsamon, patriarch of Antioch, gives the following interpretation: "This," he says, "is the difference between judges, who impose corporal punishment through their sentence, and bishops, who determine ecclesiastical punishment for penitents: that judges can neither diminish nor augment the punishment established by law without the emperor's will; bishops, who have taken upon themselves the burden of our sins through their desire to intercede with God for us, both increase and decrease punishments. For that reason, they have authority not only to shorten the period of punishment, but even to commute punishments."

Saint Gregory of Nyssa, in the fourth canon of his epistle to Bishop Letoius,[116] reasons that, when a sinner confesses his sins of his own free will while another is seized in the commission of a crime, one does not adjudge a favorable punishment to him who was seized and demonstrably accused as one does for him who voluntarily confessed.

Saint John Chrysostom, in a book on the priesthood,[117] instructs the spiritual pastor to distinguish between penitents and not equally overwhelm everyone with severe punishment. These are his words: "It is not fitting merely to impose as much punishment as possible for sins, but heed the disposition of those who have sinned, that we do not tear apart further when we wish to mend what has been torn, and that we do not lead toward a more serious downfall when we wish to raise up him who has fallen. For the greater part of mankind, weak and unrestrained, devoted to the sweetness of this life, as well as those who can boast a noble birth and preeminence over others, can, upon turning to regeneration, slowly and in small degree, even if imperfectly, at least in part, free themselves from the evils that control them. A pastor who uses punishment harshly will discourage them from amending their lives. For a soul that shame has crushed falls into despair and is neither obedient to tranquil instruction nor fearful of prohibitions; nor yet is it mollified by good works, but becomes the most wretched of that city. The Prophet, chastising such a one, says: 'You have a harlot's brow, you refuse to be ashamed.' [118] Accordingly a pastor must have much judgment and eyes without number, so that he may examine the condition of a soul from all aspects. For many reject the hope of amending their lives and succumb to despair of salvation because they are unable to endure harsh treatment. Also, conversely, a few who do not see a punishment equal to their crime give themselves to presumption and apathy, and they become more wicked than before, even more bent on sin. Therefore it is fitting to let nothing go untried, but scrutinizing all things diligently, to render expedient treatment to the person calling so that he will regard his endeavor as fruitful." Hereunto, Chrysostom.

With respect to this, that same teacher, in his first message to the erring Theodore, says briefly but clearly: "Never does God disdain repentance that is generated sincerely and with a plain heart. Even if one has reached the uttermost limits of iniquity, but wishes to return therefrom to the path of virtue, He will welcome him and embrace him compassionately. For not by length of time is repentance perfected, but only by the genuineness of the transformation."

The Council of the holy fathers *in Trullo,*[119] in canon 102, offers us reasoning similar to and much in agreement with Chrysostom's. Under that canon are these words of Patriarch Balsamon: [120] "In other synods it was determined regionally that a bishop who received the authority to loose and bind through the blessing of the Holy Ghost need not always take cognizance of the prescribed forms in the canons with respect to penance, but that he may fashion them taking into consideration the persons who are under interdict, that is to say, according to their ages, their assurances of good faith, and their initial efforts, and also taking into consideration the nature of the sin. In this way he shall give proper treatment to a person's sickness." In that same way do the Greek teachers John Zonaras [121] and Alexis Aristenos [122] explain that canon.

We conclude this with another work by Basil, who, in canon 84, speaks thus concerning the determination of penances: "All the foregoing may be interpreted in this way: that we should look upon the fruits of repentance, that we should not measure them by length of time, but form judgments according to the strength of repentance."

All these statements of our teachers instruct us sufficiently well that the canons concerning penances are not immutable, but are left to the judgment of the spiritual father, who must take notice of who the penitent is, and of what sort, whether he truly repents, and what penance he can bear, lest a severe punishment turn out to be for him the poison of despair instead of a cure. Through such examination of all circumstances, a confessor can either increase or decrease the time and the amount of penance, and substitute one penance for another. For example, a charitable donation in place of fasting, except that he ought not to require, under the appearance of charity, gifts for himself or anyone else not genuinely poor. Occasionally, upon seeing the hardship of someone in fulfilling a penance, he should impose no penance of any kind. What manner of penance, for example, can he impose on a soldier in the ranks, on a traveler in need, on a sailor, on a pauper, on a sick person, and on others like these? It is impossible for them to fast; they have nothing with which to give alms. Therefore, after having sufficiently subdued persons such as these with the fear of God's judgment, so that they will not go back to wrongdoing, the spiritual father may, for the sins that have been confessed, provided that they do truly repent, consider them worthy of forgiveness, strengthening them with the offer of God's mercy, and regard them as deserving of the Communion of the Holy Mysteries without penance. Only if a spiritual father has ascertained that the person confessing to him is one who is so ready for any penance that the penance referred to, that is, the exclusion for a certain time from the Communion of the Holy Mysteries, will not cast him either into despair or sloth and indifference, but will instead lead him to a greater understanding of the gravity of sin and God's wrath, and dispose him to a warmer repentance, to such a penitent the spiritual father may, for a certain time, together with other penances suitable for regeneration, impose also the penance of exclusion from the Holy Mysteries. However, a confessor shall not venture to carry this out by himself, but shall request a decision and permission from his bishop, after having explained to him all the circumstances surrounding the penitent, except for naming him. It is fitting henceforth to put aside, specifically and namely, the penance existing in ancient custom that deprived one of Communion for a long time. Although it was aforetime intended for the care of souls as showing the abomination of sins and restraining the evil desires of the flesh, now, however, it has not only ceased to be frightful to many, but has become desirable to indolents. It is even highly favored by secret schismatics and is purposely sought after through the confession of false sins. Consequently, for the reasons referred to and in accordance with the force of the aforementioned instructions of the Church fathers, it shall not be used.

15. When a priest comes to a sick person to hear his confession and to administer the Holy Mysteries, he shall hear his confession in private, but shall administer the Holy Mysteries in front of the people of that house and also in front of his own churchmen. This is to be done for the reason that some impious priests, concealing schismatics, pretend that they administer the Holy Mysteries to a sick person in private, so that the schismatic may be concealed by such pretended Communion. For such godlessness a priest shall be utterly estranged from the priesthood and shall be subject to a civil court for corporal punishment; and all the property of a schismatic who hides in this way shall be seized in favor of the Sovereign.

16. Whoever reports espying a priest acting illicitly in this way with a schismatic shall be given as a reward one-half or one-third part of the schismatic's confiscated property.

17. The same shall be done with a priest who, having been bought by the schismatics, accepts their children as though for baptism and sends them back without having baptized them.

18. It is a gross superstition and ostentation of certain laymen to invite priests home for the chanting of vespers, or matins, and the rest. If someone uneducated does this, it is no wonder that he is superstitious and requires correction. But if a person of reason does this, then he is exceedingly haughty, for he knows that every Christian has and ought to have the boldness, as the Apostle teaches (Heb. 10),[123] to approach God in the profession of faith and hope: "for he who has given the promise is faithful." He knows also that a priest is the director and officiator of public prayer in a house of prayer, that is, in a church of God, especially in the sacerdotal performance of the bloodless sacrifice and the other sacraments that require a priest. What can be the reason behind inviting a priest home

for chanting that can be performed without a priest? And to what purpose is there such a vast difference of influence between rich persons and their poor brethren, to whose homes priests do not come for services? In truth, this is a provocation and not a supplication to God. There happen to be in many private households fugitive priests, iniquitous and forbidden to perform priestly functions by their bishops, and impostors, while widows keep others under the appearance of church needs, not without suspicion. In spiritual matters there have been repeated instances of numerous crimes committed, irregular marriages performed,[124] etc., by priests living secretly in private households. Accordingly this disorderly custom shall be completely abandoned, and penalties shall be leveled upon those who disobey.

19. Priests, deacons, and other churchmen shall not venture to go chanting at places reputed to be miraculous that have not been accredited in a council; but they must inform their bishops and prohibit it to the people, subject to severe punishment. A priest shall not permit another priest or a hieromonk to perform the liturgy, or a hierodeacon to assist, if he does not have the attestation of a bishop that he is a regular priest or deacon and that he has been dispatched on a mission or has been given leave of absence. Likewise, during a church service, he must as far as possible tell them to stop and especially forbid them from taking part in the liturgy. Coming forth, he shall speak about this without equivocating or truckling to anyone, regardless of how high in ecclesiastical dignity the other may be.

20. A priest, because he is the pastor of those entrusted to him, must watch whether schismatic monks and teachers, or sycophants and hypocrites, enter the house of any parishioner; and should he see any, he must, under penalty of divestment of the priesthood and civil punishment,[125] seize them and send them to the house of the bishop.

21. Priests should not make a commercial enterprise from the performance of their ministry: for example, baptisms, marriages, funerals, etc., but should be satisfied with the remuneration willingly given them. This shall be especially watched with respect to the requiem service on the fortieth day after death, for which priests demand great prices even if they are not asked about it. They themselves often do not think of conducting a requiem service on the

fortieth day after death, but forcibly extort payments as though they were a duty on death. This is one evil which, if a bishop neglects to suppress it, shall furnish sufficient reason for him to be summoned to the Most Holy Ruling Synod for judgment.

22. Whereas it is His Imperial Majesty's intention to arrange the churches in such a way that a sufficient number of parishioners shall be registered at each one, and to determine what every parishioner shall owe the clergy of his church annually, so that, from their donation, all the clergy may have adequate subsistence, accordingly, in compliance with His Imperial Majesty's ukase, the Most Holy Ruling Synod, concurring with upstanding lay authorities, shall convene a council and enact the intended decree. When this has been accomplished, then priests must not thereafter seek even the smallest remuneration for the religious services that have been assigned to them unless someone should, of his own free will, wish to present some gift. But even that is not to be offered at the time when the priest is fulfilling some requirement, but after the passage of several weeks.

23. The Fourth Holy Ecumenical Council of Chalcedon, in the sixth canon, forbids the absolute ordination of priests and deacons without their becoming affiliated with a specified church, or the performance of any function related to the priesthood or the diaconate by those who are ordained in this manner. While priests and deacons in Russia are not ordained absolutely, yet many are ordained and affiliated with a single church, beyond the number of priests or deacons required; and many, having left their church, wander hither and yon, which in effect creates the same condition as absolute ordination. In order that henceforth there shall be no such disorder, laymen must not accept such priests and deacons at any kind of church service, and bishops must not ordain more than are needed. Those who have left their church, wherever such are found, shall be seized and punished. And if they should not desire to return to their churches and to serve therein in an orderly manner until death, and that under surety of honest persons, then they shall be divested of the priesthood. No superfluous priests shall be ordained under any conditions, for many are ordained and taken into the clergy who are fleeing from official duty. For this reason their number shall soon be determined by ukase.

24. If a priest or a deacon who has been divested of his ecclesias-

tical dignity by a bishop for the aforementioned crime, or for some other, should travel about the land in the guise of a priest or deacon, and undertakes to officiate at sacred services, then, after someone like this has been apprehended, he shall be sent to the Most Holy Ruling Synod, and from the Synod, he shall be referred to civil judgment. A bishop himself is free to refer such a one to civil judgment, where it is fitting.

25. But if a parish becomes so impoverished through some unavoidable exigency that it is quite impossible for a priest, together with the other churchmen, to subsist, then the bishop himself shall take care of them, not permitting them to roam, and he is to assign them where a priest is required.

26. A priest shall not, of his own accord, without his bishop's permission, venture to enlist in a military regiment, and military authorities shall not accept such persons. For violation of this, a priest shall be given over to severe punishment, and bishops shall submit written reports concerning this to the Synod as regards the military authorities (if someone among them errs in this way not on account of a priest's subterfuge, but willfully, and undertakes to defend the priest by force), and from the Synod, justice shall be sought in the Military College.[126]

27. In many churches a priest does not accept outsiders among the churchmen, but fills the vacancies of that office with his sons and kinsmen, sometimes even exceeding the need, heedless of whether they are suitable or proficient in reading and writing. This, over and above other sufficient reasons, is especially harmful because it is thereby easier for a priest to act unrestrainedly, to be unconcerned with church ritual and order, and to conceal schismatics. Article 11, mentioned above, will not be carried out by such a one. Accordingly bishops must most zealously eliminate this evil and severely punish the priests who act in violation, except that, in accordance with the decision of the parishioners and with the permission of his particular bishop, a priest may install one, and only one, of his sons, who is capable of singing and reading, as a sexton or sacristan, and the rest, who have been well educated, shall be placed in other churches or in some other honest occupation.

28. It is not enough merely to consider these other matters— whether priests, deacons, and other church people are given to disorderly conduct, whether they raise a clamor in the streets when

drunk, or what is worse, whether they are drunkenly noisome in the churches, whether they perform public church prayers in two or more parts simultaneously, whether they wrangle at meals like boors, whether they extort regalement while visiting, or whether (and this becomes intolerable shamelessness) they flaunt their bravery in fistfights: for such offenses, they shall be severely punished —but a bishop must diligently command them this, that they maintain a good personal appearance, namely, that their outer clothing, even if it is poor, be clean, and only black, not any other color, that they do not go about with their heads uncovered, that they not lie down to sleep in the streets, that they not drink in taverns, that they not display their prowess and fortitude in drinking while visiting as guests, and so on, in the same vein as this. These indecencies show them to be rogues; yet they are placed among the people as pastors and fathers.

29. Henceforth all priests shall personally be in possession of books that are customarily called *metriki,* that is, parish registry books, in which are recorded the births and baptisms of the children in their parish, designating the year and day, and naming the parents and godparents. Likewise, which children died without receiving baptism, together with an additional statement of the reason why the child was deprived of Holy Baptism. They shall also record in those books the persons of their parish who are united in matrimony. Likewise, those who die and are buried, with a statement that, in accordance with their Christian obligation, they expired in repentance; and if someone was not buried, they shall specifically state the reason why he did not receive a Christian burial, with a designation of the year and day. These books shall be declared to the Episcopal Chancery annually; how many are born and die shall be reported to the Episcopal Chanceries every four months, and written notification concerning that shall be made from the Episcopal Chanceries to the Synod.

30. There must be thorough study in the Most Holy Ruling Synod about what to do with widowed priests and deacons, especially those who have been widowed in youth.

There existed heretofore the custom of making them monks; but how can such a one pronounce before God the pledge that he does not enter the monastic life out of need? What if he does not feel this vocation in himself and does not especially desire it? It is not necessary to force them, but they may be tonsured and placed on probation if they are freely willing.

ON MONKS

The monastic life in particular, which in ancient times was for all Christendom like a mirror and model of repentance and rectitude, has in these times become corrupted through many irregularities. Accordingly the following rules shall serve for its correction.

Whom To Accept as Monks and How

1. A person less than thirty years of age shall not be accepted as a monk. It is not sufficient for the monastic life for a person to have attained complete reason, but he must have an understanding of his own nature, whether he does have a vocation for the celibate life.

2. A soldier shall not be accepted, for it is evident that such a one does not come forward with a monastic intention, but sins exceedingly, fleeing from his duty. This is glaring disobedience of the supreme authority's command, and brings harm to the entire state. If anyone is given dispensation for this by the highest authority, then he may be accepted following three years' probation.

3. A strange peasant shall not be accepted unless he has a leave of absence letter from his landlord. But even so, it shall be observed who he is and of what sort, what his age is, whether there is any forgery, and one should first inquire why he was released by his landlord, and whether he is literate. Those who are illiterate shall, most emphatically, not be tonsured except by the personal ukase of His Imperial Majesty and the decree of the Synod.

4. A man shall not be accepted who has a wife living. There exists a custom in which a husband and wife undertake a mutual agreement that the husband will be tonsured as a monk, but the wife will be free to go after another. This divorce appears correct to simple people, but it is utterly repugnant to the word of God if it is undertaken for this reason alone. But even if there were sufficient reason for divorce, husband and wife nevertheless shall not perform it of their own volition, but shall make representation in detail concerning that divorce to their bishop, who, after having examined the matter carefully, shall write to the Most Holy Ruling Synod for consideration and a determination, and he shall not effect such divorces if he has not received decisions from the Synod.

5. But if a husband and wife have expressed the desire in their mutual agreement to enter the monastic life, then, besides the other circumstances, the age of the wife shall be noted, whether she is past fifty years, or sixty, and whether they have children, and how they are leaving them.

6. Let it be known to all—and archimandrites and hegumens must tell this to sons who come to enter the monastic life without their parents' permission, also to parents who bind a child to the monastic life, to husbands who leave their wives, and to wives who leave their husbands—that it is odious to God to leave their own in this way, as though for Christ's sake, without comprehending the meaning of the Lord's words: "For this cause a man shall leave his father and mother," [127] etc. For Our Lord spoke about necessary, and not willful, separation, that is, if it should be impossible for someone to love Christ while living together with parents or children, with husband or wife, then a person must forsake that life together, and prefer the love of God over the love of his own. This happens, for example, if an infidel parent does not allow his son to maintain Christian piety, or if he is in the faith, yet he impels him to some misdeed; or if it is impossible to live with parents, or with a wife, because of cruel persecution by infidels and it is impossible to flee with one's wife, or parents, and others. But contrary to this was the speculation of the heretic, Eustathius of Sebaste,[128] who taught simply to leave children and parents and husbands and wives, as if that very abandonment were pleasing to God. This teaching was anathematized at the Council of the holy fathers in Gangra.

7. It shall be diligently observed with respect to him who enters the monastic life that he is not bound by indebtedness, that he is not fleeing from judgment for theft, or whether there is any of the Sovereign's business pursuant to him, or anything similar. Such as these do not repent, but seek to hide, and occasion great misfortune for a monastery. To prevent this, monks coming from another eparchy, and unknown to honest people, shall not be accepted.

8. Officials from central administrative agencies [129] shall not be accepted without a leave of absence letter from a governor [130] or a voivode,[131] or from a bishop or a monastery, with the affixture of their signatures and with an attestation that such persons are freed from administrative duties. This shall likewise be understood as applying to town administrators.[132]

9. Among certain people, it has become the custom that parents bind their young sons to the monastic life even before they have reached the age of reason; later they exhort and impel them, having come of age, to become tonsured as monks, recalling to them their promise and not permitting them to marry. This custom is spiritually baneful both for the children and the parents. Because it is a life imposed upon the children by necessity, it is a sinful affliction, and the parents will be guilty of that sin. Although children are subject to their parents' will, they are nevertheless not like dumb beasts in that respect, especially in what requires their judgment and volition, such as one's choice of life. This shall be rigorously watched, and those who are thus bound and coerced shall not be tonsured [133] and shall not be accepted.

10. This is a frivolous and vain custom: Someone gives a donation of several rubles to a monastery, thereby placing the monastery under an obligation, so that, whenever he desires, he will be accepted into the monastic life. Then he enters the monastery as if into his own patrimonial estate. There he seeks accommodation in consideration of his donation as though for some debt, and by complaining extorts it from the prior. There is a general feeling that such a one must not be excluded from the monastic life. Henceforth such donations and donators shall not be accepted. But if someone does accept, he shall be expelled from the priorship.

11. When such a one appears for whom not one of these precautions constitutes an impediment to the monastic life, then, nevertheless, after he has been accepted into the monastery, he shall not be tonsured precipitately, but he shall be given over to an honest and sober elder, with whom, and under whose supervision, he shall live. He shall receive the common monasterial duties, whichever the prior may prescribe; and thus, in humility and temperance, he shall remain at the monastery, without leaving, for three years. Every year he shall go to confession and receive the Holy Mysteries at least four times, during the four fasts. This will show who does insincerely and who does in honesty select the monastic life. For truly zealous toilers will not refuse a three-year probation, whereas those who dissimulate will not be able to persevere and, hence, will not attain to monkhood.

12. Yet even one who has thus undergone a three-year probation shall not be tonsured without the bishop's permission; but the archi-

mandrite or hegumen, together with his confessor and the elder who supervised him theretofore, shall present him, testifying before the bishop concerning him, that he sincerely desires monkhood and that, having remained three years in the monastery, he is meek, humble, patient, obedient, and sober. This testimony shall be given and recorded in writing. Then the bishop, having instructed him, shall permit him to be tonsured. If that monastery should be at a far distance from a bishop, then the written testimony concerning such persons shall be sent to the bishop with the signatures of the prior and the brethren.

13. Before tonsuring, he shall be given to read, and if he is not lettered, then he shall have read to him, questions and answers with respect to tonsuring, so that he may judge what promise he will have to pronounce and whether he is able to live by the promise. Likewise he shall be read the rules written herein. But better is it still to read all this to him often throughout his three-year probation.

14. If it happens that, after all his three-year probation and also after the testimony before the bishop, he demurs and does not desire to become a monk, then he shall be freely released without any restraint or reproach.

15. If, having left, he again should desire to return to that same monastery, or wish to be tonsured in another, then he shall undergo the three-year probation anew.

16. If someone should desire to give a donation to a monastery, it shall not be accepted from him except following the three-year probation, and then provided that he signs a statement that he does not seek any privilege on account of that donation and that he will not boast and talk about it to the prior and the brethren, that he will not even remember it, but will completely erase it as though he had never given anything.

On the Monks' Life

17. They must go to confession and receive the Holy Mysteries four times a year during the four holy fasts; and more often would be fitting, for the most perfect life is glorified by these sacraments. In the early Church, all Christians frequently went to Communion, and a liturgy never took place but that there were communicants, as we see at the present time in the words of the Divine Liturgy: "Holy things unto the Holy; [134] in the fear of God and with faith

draw near," [135] etc. And Saint Chrysostom greatly impugns noncommunicants.

18. Priors, always designating for them some task, shall most emphatically not allow monks to be idle. But it would be better to initiate in the monasteries arts and crafts: for example, joinery, iconography, etc., whatever is not contrary to monasticism; and for nuns, spinning, sewing, making lace, etc.

19. No one shall have servants except directors and the elderly, but even for directors, not more than necessary. There should be regular infirmaries for the elderly and the sick, and attendants shall be assigned there in proportion.

20. No monk shall, of his own accord, invite guests to visit him, either purposely for feasting or even for calling on the way from church, except with the prior's permission; and there should be with the guests another honest brother, whom the prior shall appoint.

21. A monk shall not go visiting without the prior's permission, and then not alone, but with another honest elder. He shall not go more often than four times a year, except in emergencies, and then not without the prior's permission. For the sake of precluding all suspicion, monks shall not, under any conditions, subject to severe punishment, go to the homes of laymen, much less to nunneries, without a respectable reason, which, in virtue of a most irreproachable requirement, it is no longer possible to avoid.

22. As with edibles, so with other items, monks shall not sell monasterial articles, even though they have been issued to them, either in the city streets, in the monastery, or indeed, anywhere at all, for this is an utterly shameful and extremely dishonest practice.

23. After the refection the prior and brethren shall never take to their cells food left over from the meal, except quass,[136] for otherwise, everything may be dissipated uselessly outside the monastery.

24. None of the brethren, or the prior, is to take his meals alone in his cell, but only in the common refectory, except out of genuine infirmity or for other respectable reasons.

25. Food, drink, and clothing shall be equally distributed to all. Otherwise everyone will try to steal extra items of food, drink, and clothing. However, clothes shall be differentiated, one kind for those attending at the altar, another for those who serve, upon determination.

26. No one shall have the authority to give anything away from

the monastery, except the prior, and then with an announcement to the elder brethren: specifically, with written notification as to whom and upon what occasion it was given. Otherwise everyone will shamelessly attempt to distribute monasterial property among relatives and friends. Thus we shall eschew sin and needless losses, and instead of ten brothers, thirty can be maintained.

27. It is fitting that communal life exist in the monasteries according to the rules of the holy fathers; otherwise, if there is no communal life, everyone will individually fetch whatever he needs.

28. All the revenues accruing from monasterial landed estates, those received as donations from God-loving persons, and church revenues shall be received in a single designated place, wherefrom they shall be utilized for all the needs of the Church, the monastery, and the brethren. Otherwise there will be no end to impropriation of property arising out of a lust for power, which is truly ruinous for cloisters and enriching for the kinsmen of those therein, on account of which unworthy persons, anxiously forestalling one another, grasp for the diaconate, the priesthood, and the rest of the directorate, whatever is its rank.

29. No one in a monastery shall keep extraneous money and belongings, except books. Whereas this gives occasion to pride and the pursuit of pleasure, many enter a monastery with those ends in mind under the appearance of suffering. If anything is found to be kept by someone, openly or secretly, it shall be taken to the monastery's treasury.

30. In accordance with the injunction of the holy fathers, monks shall absolutely not be permitted to transfer from monastery to monastery, unless there are respectable reasons, and then only with a dimissory letter from the prior. For primarily on account of this, obedience, patience, and humility have, contrary to monastic vows, been uprooted, and every kind of virulence and wickedness is assuming enormous force. For on account of this, many unordained persons carry out sacred functions; others, excommunicated by their bishops and confessors, function likewise, again without permission; many who walk about dressed in the manner of monks are untonsured. From these things arise all kinds of evils to tempt many and to bring considerable disgrace upon every favorable aspect of the monasteries, the good order of the Church, and due reverence for monasticism.

31. Monks shall not go from a monastery into cities or villages, except out of some common requirement. He who sets out upon this shall be chosen by common vote, and he shall proceed upon the errand with a written leave of absence granted by the prior.

32. For those monks who are sent to a different eparchy and to the capital upon some mission, it is not enough that they have a written leave of absence from their prior, but they must have a written leave of absence from their bishop. Wherever a monk appears without a written leave of absence, he shall be seized and sent to the bishop of that place where he appears; and in the capital, such monks shall be sent to the Most Holy Ruling Synod. Vagrant monks are to be sought out by those whom the Senate will establish, as well as by citizens.[137]

33. Should it happen that someone from among the clergy or the laity undertakes to protect such monks, then those protectors shall be notified that they must produce the monk at a specified place, and a written report about this shall be made immediately to the Most Holy Ruling Synod.

34. Women shall never be allowed in the cells of the prior or the brethren, with the exception of the guests' cell, and even there not privately, but in the presence of venerable monks who shall be designated for this. In this way every deprecation and reproach forthcoming from foreigners and from our own people shall be utterly quashed, except for that which it is impossible to avoid in this regard.

35. In all monasteries it is fitting to teach monks not only so that they can read what is written, but so that they will be able to understand. For this, a cell shall be specially established, and selected monks, who know the meaning of the Divine Scriptures, shall be appointed thereto in order that they may thus choose educated persons who are worthy of the priesthood and of every position of authority.

36. Monks shall not, for anyone's benefit, write in their cells any notes, such as excerpts from books, or letters of advice, without the personal knowledge of their prior, subject to severe corporal punishment; and they shall not receive letters except with the permission of the prior. In accordance with the spiritual and civil regulations, they shall not keep ink and paper, except that which is specially permitted by the prior for general spiritual use. This shall be dili-

gently watched among the monks, for nothing so undoes monastic silence as their frivolous and vain writings. But if there arises for a brother the genuine necessity of writing, he shall write in the refectory from the common inkwell and on common paper, by special permission from the prior, and he shall not venture to do that of his own accord, subject to severe punishment.[138]

On Nuns

All the aforementioned rules concerning monks must be kept also by nuns, and in addition, they shall keep these special ones.

37. Never, under any circumstances, shall nuns go to men's monasteries or to parish churches on feast days, neither during processions of the cross. They shall not visit nunneries, except for the hegumena, with one or two sisters, whom she shall select, accompanying her. Nunneries shall always be kept locked except during respectable times, such as the Holy Liturgy, or for seemly persons, such as a confessor for the need of the sick.[139] Whereas almost all nunneries have churches just inside the gates, a porch shall be built onto the church, where it is appropriate, leading into the street; and there shall be one set of doors leading from the church into the nunnery, and those shall open into the hegumena's cell. If somewhere there are relics, etc., because of which people have been largely accustomed to come, then they shall be transferred close by the gate, so that none shall find any pretense for entering the nunnery. For the sake of precluding suspicion, no one, either laymen or monks, shall ever be permitted to go about the cells; and that, most emphatically, shall be strictly prohibited.

38. If the need arises for a nunnery to seek justice against someone in a secular tribunal, the nuns shall not go forth for that litigation, but they shall send a pleader, or they may request the bishop that he send someone to represent them.

39. Should an urgent matter arise involving the capital city, the nuns shall request their bishop that he write about it to the Most Holy Ruling Synod; but he shall not give them leave to go.

40. Nuns shall not live in laic houses, nor shall they roam about the land for any need. Excepted from this is His Tsarist Majesty's family.

41. Nuns shall not mingle in their church with the people, but

some shall be selected to sing in the choir, while the rest shall remain in the rear,[140] where they shall stand alone.

42. As the Apostle commanded with regard to the selection of widows, "Let a widow," he said, "who is selected be not less than sixty years old" (Tim. 5),[141] the same shall also be kept as regards the taking of the veil by nuns, except in accordance with some special determination of the Synod.

43. Should some young girl desire to remain a virgin with the intention of taking monastic orders, then, after examining diligently whether she is not selecting the celibate life insincerely, out of some need or weakness or dissimulation, such a one shall be given over to an honest and well-secured nunnery under the supervision of a trustworthy and constant elder nun. Then the girl shall remain without orders until she is sixty, or at least fifty, years old.

On Monasteries

44. Monks shall not be allowed to build hermitages in the wilderness. Many do this for the sake of a free life, so as to live removed from all authority and supervision, according to one's own will, and so that the newly founded hermitage may collect money and profit thereby. Yet such a monk deprives himself of great spiritual benefit: he does not have whom to ask for spiritual counsel, for an answer to doubtful notions and perplexing moral questions; he does not see the example of other monks' strivings. What, then, when the hour of death overtakes him in such isolation? Who will minister to him in his sickness? Who will comfort, instruct, and strengthen him against desperate fear? And not as an example to us is the eremetical life of the early fathers, such as Paul of Thebes,[142] Anthony the Great,[143] Macarius of Egypt,[144] etc., for then men were well-versed in Christian theology and possessed great discernment and proficiency. For an ignorant person, such a life is dangerous and subject to soul-shattering calamity. Furthermore, because of the cold climate, it is impossible for a true hermitage to exist in Russia. In Palestine and other warm countries,[145] there are adequate fruits by which to subsist, and thus it is possible, in great measure, to remove oneself from the world. Here it is impossible to live without plowland, fishing, or kitchen gardens, which cannot exist secretly and in isolation.

45. It is fitting to combine monasteries in which there are few

brethren into a single cloister, where there will be enough of them so that they can subsist. However, out of very necessity, for the sake of better devotions, there shall not be less than thirty brothers. Since it is impossible for a small brotherhood to observe daily divine service and communal life as it is fitting, for that reason such monasteries remain to a large degree without church service, as if empty. Henceforth secular priests and deacons shall absolutely not be assigned to men's monasteries; and the monasterial churches that have been left shall be converted into parish churches, and the priest and churchmen shall be given a substantial part of that monastery's land. What remains shall be assigned to that same monastery to which the brethren shall be transferred. And if this will be implemented in accordance with this plan, then, assuredly, in all the holy churches (of which there are not more than three kinds that it is suitable to have in every monastery: namely, cathedral, refectory, and infirmary) [146] there shall be daily service in the cloisters, besides devotions, community life, and every favorable monastic feature, by reason of the multitude of the brethren. And in those that remain as parish churches, there shall also be daily service because parish priests shall be appointed in keeping with actual need. The brethren, through the union of the common monasterial landed estates and other revenues, shall receive everything in greater abundance for themselves with respect to all their needs rather than, as before, suffering privation and having disorder in everything because of a small [147] brotherhood. Likewise shall this be implemented with regard to nunneries.

46. Moreover, at the time when all former monasterial landed estates, together with the revenues, will be transferred to those monasteries that have great abundance with which to meet their needs, there shall, at those monasteries, be constructed hospitals, or lazarettos, and it shall be directed that there be gathered therein, upon examination, those who are advanced in years and those who are in exceedingly poor health, those who are unable to subsist by themselves, and those who have no one to care for them, so that such persons, to the glory of God, may be provided with all necessities of retreat in a manner similar to that indicated in the *Naval Regulation* [148] as regards the establishment of such retreat.

47. Such construction as occurs in monasteries that exceeds the need through superfluity, as it is not to the glory of God, shall not

be permitted; but it shall be commanded to use the available resources for a hospital, and such a work will be more pleasing before God as being a necessary construction.

48. No one shall build new monasteries, either men's or women's, without the knowledge of the Most Holy Ruling Synod.

On Priors of Monasteries

49. It is fitting to select for the spiritual directorate men of good morals and versed in the monastic life, irreproachable and certified, having a good understanding of Scripture and the rule of monasterial and monastic life, so that they will care for the salvation of the brethren's souls and not just for the construction of walls and the accumulation of much wealth, and so that they will govern boldly, yet cautiously, according to their calling. To that end, every prior, before his appointment to the directorate shall be administered an oath, duly confirmed.

50. If, following his selection, a spiritual director, contrary to his calling, does not undertake to be solicitous, as becomes a pastor, for the salvation of the souls entrusted to him in pastoral care, such a one, without delay, shall be relegated to the lowest monastic degree, and in his place, at the council of the brethren, another shall be selected. The others who are placed in authority shall, upon seeing these things, be circumspect, and the monasterial regulatory articles shall be well and wholly observed.

51. If some prior, of his own accord, receives a fugitive monk without an ukase, such a one shall be relegated, until his death, to monasterial labor, and furthermore, such a one shall never be a director.

52. Escaped monks shall be kept at monasterial toils in fetters until death.

53. In every monastery there shall be a registry book. In it, under the signature of the director, shall be inscribed the time and name of a monk's taking orders, and of what class he was in the world.

54. The monastery's treasury shall not be in the prior's cell, nor shall it be kept under his key only, but also under the treasurer's key, in a special place and under the monastery's seal; similarly, the church sacristy.

55. Once a week, or at least once a month, the prior and the cellarer, in the presence of several other most upstanding elders, shall

audit the monastery's revenues and expenditures, and having audited them, they shall record them in a book, so that the prior can give to the one to whom he is subordinate an accounting of it.

56. A prior shall not compel the brethren to come to him for confession, as such a confession would be a sham.

57. There shall be in a monastery a single common confessor, a hieromonk certified before the bishop. He should from time to time tell the prior if some evil practice has taken root among the brethren. However, he shall not mention the persons by name, indicate their cells, or refer to any other circumstances. Thus a prior can determine and seek earnestly as to how that evil can be eradicated within the monastery. The same shall be observed with respect to a confessor in nunneries.

58. If a prior, having accepted a bribe, gives testimony to a bishop about someone who desires to become a monk, saying that he is suited to that life, such a one shall be divested of his authority and reduced to a common monk.

59. A prior shall not keep relatives with him, nor shall he assign them to monasterial tasks. Likewise this shall not be permitted to others from among the brethren, and bishops should not do this in their houses except for respectable reasons, as when, because of old age, more efficient service can be rendered by one of their own kinsmen than by an outsider.

60. No valuables of any kind shall be accepted in monasteries for safekeeping either by the brethren or by the prior.

61. Upon the death of bishops, archimandrites, hegumens, and others of monastic rank, nothing of their personal property shall be given to their kinsmen by birth or marriage; but of such articles, those belonging to the higher ranks shall be sent to the Most Holy Ruling Synod, while those belonging to the lower ranks shall be gathered in the monastery's treasury.

62. All these listed rules, and any that may be newly issued by the Most Holy Ruling Synod, shall be read in all monasteries once a month, on Sundays, in the refectory, lest anyone excuse himself through ignorance.[149]

Concerning these things, many canons, composed of old by saints, and statutes, established by imperial laws, are to be found in the *Book of the Rudder* [150] and likewise in the conciliar interpretation of the Most Holy Patriarchs of Alexandria, Antioch, and Moscow, and of many Greek and all the Russian bishops, rendered in the year 7175 since the creation of the world, 1667 since the Birth of Christ.[151]

His Imperial Majesty himself was pleased to hear, in His Own High Person, this Supplement to the *Spiritual Regulation* and to make corrections in his own hand; and having approved everything that has been written, he has prescribed, in the latter days of April and the first days of May of this year, 1722, that it be published and promulgated.[152]

Notes

Introduction

1. Translation of *Dukhovnyi reglament.* The original draft of this document bore a lengthy descriptive title as part of the opening paragraph, beginning as follows: *Kniga siia Dukhovnago Kollegium opisanie i razsuzhdenie soderzhashchaia . . .* [This Book, which Contains a Description of and a Treatise on the Spiritual College . . .]; see note 7 of the present translation. That title was changed after the document was revised and enacted into law. It then read, in part: *Reglament ili Ustav Dukhovnogo Kollegium . . .* [The Regulation or Statute of the Spiritual College . . .]. See P. V. Verkhovskoi, *Uchrezhdenie Dukhovnoi kollegii i Dukhovnyi reglament. K voprosu ob otnoshenii Tserkvi i gosudarstva v Rossii* [The Establishment of the Spiritual College and the Spiritual Regulation. On the Question of the Relations of Church and State in Russia], 2, pt. 1: 27. The latter title (*Reglament . . .*) was retained with slight variations (in the genitive-singular case forms of the adjective-noun combination denoting the Spiritual College, viz.: (1) *Dukhovnoi Kollegii;* (2) *Dukhovnyia Kollegii*) when the document was printed in *Polnoe sobranie zakonov Rossiiskoi imperii s 1649 goda* [The Complete Collection of the Laws of the Russian Empire from 1649], 6:314–46, no. 3718, wherein also were included the Manifesto of 25 January 1721 and the Oath of the Members of the Spiritual College.

The present translation of the Manifesto of 25 January 1721, the Oath of the Members of the Spiritual College, the *Spiritual Regulation,* and the Supplement to the *Spiritual Regulation* is based on the aforementioned text printed in *Polnoe sobranie zakonov,* compared, corrected, and amplified on the basis of the superbly edited version published by Verkhovskoi (*Uchrezhdenie,* 2, pt. 1:3–105) and the less definitive, but still useful, compilation produced by V. N. Beneshevich (*Sbornik pamiatnikov po istorii tserkovnago prava, preimushchestvenno*

[35]

Russkoi Tserkvi do epokhi Petra Velikago [A Collection of Monuments on the History of Ecclesiastical Law, Principally of the Russian Church to the Period of Peter the Great], 2:89–155; 159–191).

In place of its long title, the basic document has customarily been called *Dukhovnyi reglament.* This title has been variously translated into English: e.g., "Ecclesiastical Regulation" by James Cracraft, *The Church Reform of Peter the Great,* pp. ix–311 passim; "Church Regulation" by Alexander Lipski, "A Re-examination of the Dark Era of Anna Ioannovna," p. 477; "Spiritual Rule" by Alexander Schmemann, *The Historical Road of Eastern Orthodoxy,* pp. 333 ff. William K. Medlin abbreviated the title and left it in transliterated form, "Reglament," in *Moscow and East Rome,* pp. 219 ff. In the first volume of *Anthology of Russian Literature,* edited by Leo Wiener, pp. 212–14, the title "Spiritual Reglement" is employed, and a portion of the text (the first nine paragraphs in the section "Teachers and Students in Educational Institutions; So Also Church Preachers") has been translated into English.

The rendering of the title in the present translation follows that used in the first, and only other complete, English translation of the *Dukhovnyi reglament:* that of Thomas Consett, *The Present State and Regulations of the Church of Russia,* vol. 1. It also accords with the English-language version admitted into Petrine histories of both older and more recent vintage, including: Ian Grey, *Peter the Great, Emperor of All Russia,* p. 505; L. J. Oliva, *Russia in the Era of Peter the Great,* pp. 139–40; Eugene Schuyler, *Peter the Great, Emperor of Russia: A Study of Historical Biography,* 2:395; Benedict H. Sumner, *Peter the Great and the Emergence of Russia,* p. 144.

The closest alternatives to the word "spiritual" in the title of the present work are "ecclesiastical" or "church." However, these alternatives have been deliberately rejected. Strictly speaking it is the Russian word *tserkovnyi,* not *dukhovnyi,* that should be translated "ecclesiastical" or "church." And this distinction has a historical basis. For example, at the beginning of the eighteenth century, *tserkovnyi* was used in contradistinction to *dukhovnyi* to refer to that large body of unordained ecclesiastical persons (*tserkovnago prichta liudi*), such as church secretaries, sextons, etc., who performed numerous administrative, custodial, and supportive tasks at the parish level. In the present translation they are variously referred to as "church people" or "churchmen." In contrast the word *dukhovnyi* was reserved for the clergy. Thus the translation of *dukhovnyi* by "ecclesiastical" or "church" is not wholly accurate. Of course it is difficult and artificial to try to reproduce these distinctions exactly and consistently in English. Clergymen, after all, are commonly referred to (as indeed they are in this translation) as "ecclesiastics," "churchmen," etc., and it would be doing violence to contemporary English to call them by a makeshift calque, such as "spiritual persons."

There are, nevertheless, two additional arguments in favor of the word "spiritual" as an element in the translation of the title *Dukhovnyi reglament*. First, it embodies a certain ambiguity that mirrors the literalness of the original, for the ambiguity is present in Russian as well as English. Secondly, the ambiguity is a serviceable one. For in the present translation the word "spiritual" is intended to connote matters pertaining either specifically to church administration or to norms of religious practice in a more general sense. It is hoped by its use to avoid the narrower institutional orientation imparted by such titles as "Ecclesiastical Regulation," "Church Regulation," "Clerical Regulation," and so on. The word "spiritual" as employed here, then, is meant to suggest the fundamental thesis developed more fully in the present introduction: that the document under consideration concerns not only the establishment and functioning of a particular ecclesiastical administration, but that it also bears upon the prescription by an authority other than ecclesiastical of standards determined to be valid by that same other authority for governing the conduct of religious life whether within or without the parameters of any given ecclesiastical organization.

As for the second element of the title, "regulation" seems less forced than the combination of the English "spiritual" with either a direct borrowing of the French *règlement* or its Russian derivative, *reglament*. Certainly no sacrifice of precision is incurred by adopting the more familiar form. Its use in place of "rule" achieves the effect of not attributing ecclesiastical, and particularly monastic, origination to the term.

2. Official records of the Senate indicate that in St. Petersburg the actual signing of the *Spiritual Regulation* by bishops, archimandrites, and Senators took place on 27 February 1720. See S. G. Runkevich, *Istoriia Russkoi Tserkvi pod upravleniem sviatieishago sinoda* [The History of the Russian Church under the Administration of the Most Holy Synod], p. 122.

3. *Pribavlenie k Dukhovnomu reglamentu*, the present translation of which is based on the text contained in *Polnoe sobranie zakonov*, 6:699–715, no. 4022. After Peter had signed the *Spiritual Regulation* and before it was published as a legal enactment on 16 September 1721, the signed text underwent revision and was considerably expanded by the addition of the Supplement to the *Spiritual Regulation*. The two documents, constituting, in effect, a single enactment (Verkhovskoi, *Uchrezhdenie*, 1:x–xi, 195), were issued for distribution and sale together. However, possibly because Peter had not yet approved the Supplement for publication, further circulation of the Supplement, together with the *Spiritual Regulation*, was discontinued at some time between 16 September and 19 November 1721 (Verkhovskoi, *Uchrezhdenie*, 1:198), and either the Supplement alone, or the Supplement and the *Spiritual Regulation*, may have been withdrawn from circulation. The specific reasons behind Peter's discontinuance of the circulation of the *Spiritual Regulation* and the Supplement remain unclear. Some tentative solutions are suggested by Verkhovskoi, *Uchrezhdenie*, 1:202–6. At any rate, on 23 February 1722, a second edition of the *Spiritual Regula-*

tion, without the Supplement, was printed, but held back temporarily from distribution.

As for the Supplement, Verkhovskoi has admirably traced its tortuous path to publication. First of all an exact manuscript copy of the first printed version was made to be submitted to Peter for his personal examination and correction. This rather curious procedure was followed because it was considered improper to present the tsar with a printed copy for this purpose. Beginning in November 1721, then, Peter used this manuscript copy to correct and expand the Supplement. Assisting him were Prokopovich and perhaps at times the rest of the Synod. The revision continued at least until the end of April or the beginning of May 1722. It was then, according to the last sentence in the final edition of the Supplement, that Peter approved the corrected draft and prescribed its publication and promulgation (see p. 84 of the present translation).

However, according to Verkhovskoi, the process of revision may have continued even beyond that date. For Article 11 of the Supplement contains reference to the synodal announcement of 17 May 1722 (see p. 62 and n. 112 of the present translation). Since Peter had left Saint Petersburg to undertake his Persian campaign on 13 May 1722, he could not have been present when this addition was made to the text of the Supplement. This suggests that he entrusted Feofan Prokopovich to carry the document through its final stages of preparation for the press. These final stages were concluded on an unspecified day in May 1722 when the Most Holy Synod concurred in harmony (*soglasno prigovorili*) with the tsar's prescription to print the Supplement. On 14 June 1722 the Supplement was printed in Moscow and bound together with the 23 February 1722 printed edition of the *Spiritual Regulation.*

However, this did not end the matter. Before the documents could be put into circulation, the Synod was given reason to believe that Peter still had misgivings about certain portions of the text. Consequently the combined *Spiritual Regulation* and its Supplement were once more withheld from release. Only after the Synod had made sure of its footing by again receiving permission from the tsar did it issue an order for the documents to be distributed and offered for sale. This took place on 28 September 1722.

For a detailed enumeration of the editions of the *Spiritual Regulation* and its Supplement, and of their previous translations into various languages, together with a description of the circumstances surrounding their publication, see Verkhovskoi, *Uchrezhdenie,* 1:195–221.

It may be noted that, if Verkhovskoi's account is correct, then certain details recently presented by G. L. Bissonnette in "Pufendorf and the Church Reforms of Peter the Great" are in error.

On p. 97 Bissonnette states: "The complete text [of the *Spiritual Regulation*] had been read in the Senate and subscribed by Peter, the senators and the members of the Russian Orthodox hierarchy who were present in Petersburg at the time. This was on February 14, 1721, and a number of months then elapsed while the signatures of the other bishops and monastic superiors were collected." However, in the closing statement of the *Spiritual Regulation* (see the present translation, p. 56), 23 February 1720 is given as the date on which the event referred to took place (although the signing probably occurred on 27 February). 14 February 1721 marked the date on which the Spiritual College first convened and on which it received the name "Most Holy Ruling Synod." The collection of the signatures of bishops and other ecclesiastical dignitaries by Lieutenant Colonel Semen Davydov took place between 18 or 20 March 1720 and 4 January 1721 (Verkhovskoi, *Uchrezhdenie,* 1:175).

On p. 98: After the distribution of the *Spiritual Regulation* and the Supplement had been halted, Peter ". . . then proceeded to delete two chapters from the Regulation." However, Verkhovskoi indicates that Peter actually made only two minor revisions in the text, while many new provisions were added (*Uchrezhdenie,* 1:199).

On p. 98: "This truncated text was printed and released on November 19, 1721." At this point there is a footnote referring to N. A. Voskresensky, ed., *Zakonodatel'nye akty Petra I* [The Legislative Acts of Peter I], 1:198. However, there is nothing in the cited reference that pertains to the subject under discussion. It may have been intended that the note refer to Verkhovskoi, *Uchrezhdenie,* 1:198; but if that is the case, then the details offered by Verkhovskoi have been misconstrued. For there was, according to him, no text of the *Spiritual Regulation* or Supplement printed for release on 19 November 1721. Rather, on that date, the Synod directed that there be sent immediately a copy of the *Spiritual Regulation* to the Senate. It is on the basis of this occurrence that Verkhovskoi is led to assume that it was at some time between 16 September and 19 November 1721 that the distribution of the *Spiritual Regulation* was interrupted, the Supplement having been already brought under question by Peter.

On p. 98: "The omitted chapters were restored and the complete text distributed on December 19, 1722." Here another reference is made to Voskresensky, *Zakonodatel'nye akty,* 1:100. However, the reference is again not pertinent: quoted therein is an ukase of 19 March 1722, whose provisions (on various matters, chiefly the establishment and administration of lazarettos) Peter wished to have incorporated into the Supplement. Verkhovskoi mentions no text of the *Spiritual Regulation* or Supplement that was issued on 19 December 1722. A third edition of the *Regulation,* corresponding in all respects to the second, was issued on 18 January 1723.

4. The question of the selection, interpretation, and presentation of issues in writing the history of the Russian Church is discussed by

Georges Florovsky, in his review of "Ocherki po istorii Russkoi Tserkvi" [Essays on the History of the Russian Church] by A. V. Kartashev, p. 575.

5. Schmemann, *The Historical Road,* p. 335. For a survey of the Russian Church during this period, see A. V. Kartashev, *Ocherki po istorii Russkoi Tserkvi,* 2:311–20.

6. Georges Florovsky, *Puti russkago bogosloviia* [The Paths of Russian Theology], p. 92.

7. Ibid. The specific doctrines at issue, based on Prokopovich's writings in Russian and Latin, were set forth by Stefan Iavorsky in a letter to two bishops. The letter has been published under the title "Poslanie Stefana Iavorskago, mitropolita riazanskago i muromskago, . . . ob uchenii ieromonakha Feofana Prokopovicha" [The Epistle of Stefan Iavorsky, metropolitan of Riazan' and Murom, . . . on the Teaching of Hieromonk Feofan Prokopovich], pp. 5–8. For a discussion of Prokopovich's religious views, see A. V. Kartashev, "K voprosu o pravoslavii Feofana Prokopovicha" [On the Question of the Orthodoxy of Feofan Prokopovich], pp. 225–36.

8. Thomas M. Parker, *Christianity and the State in the Light of History,* p. 166.

9. Ibid.

10. Florovsky, *Puti,* p. 87.

11. Ibid.

12. The crucial phrase *"dlia podpisaniia"* was contained in an order from the Senate, date 9 March 1720, issued in compliance with an ukase from the tsar (Verkhovskoi, *Uchrezhdenie,* 1:173–78). See also Runkevich, *Istoriia Russkoi Tserkvi,* p. 121.

13. When the bishops of Chernigov and Pereiaslavl' hesitated signing, the Senate resolved, on 14 August 1720, to order the governor of Kiev to dispatch them to Saint Petersburg (Verkhovskoi, *Uchrezhdenie,* 1:178).

14. On the changes brought about by Peter's ecclesiastical reform in the relations between the Russian church and the other Eastern Orthodox churches, see ibid., 1:661–83. For the Russian and Greek texts of Peter's announcement, dated 30 September 1721, to Jeremiah, patriarch of Constantinople, and through him to the other patriarchs of the Orthodox church, concerning the establishment of the "Spiritual Synod," see Beneshevich, *Sbornik,* 2:206–12. The history of the jurisdictional relations between the patriarch of Constantinople and the Russian church to 1685 is traced by T. Barsov in *Konstantinopol'skii patriarkh i ego vlast' nad Russkoiu Tserkoviu* [The Patriarch of Constantinople and His Authority Over the Russian Church].

15. N. F. Kapterev, *Patriarkh Nikon i Tsar' Aleksiei Mikhailovich* [Patriarch Nikon and Tsar Alexis Mikhailovich], 2:244 (hereafter cited as *Nikon i Aleksiei*).

16. Verkhovskoi, *Uchrezhdenie,* 1:11.

17. Kapterev, *Nikon i Aleksiei,* 2:115.
18. Ibid.
19. Ibid.
20. Ibid., 2:54.
21. Ibid., 2:59.
22. Ibid., 2:116.
23. Ibid., 2:61.
24. A. Ia. Shpakov, "Gosudarstvo i tserkov v ikh vzaimnykh otno-sheniiakh v Moskovskom gosudarstvie. Uchrezhcenie patriarshestva v Rossii" [State and Church in Their Mutual Relations in the Muscovite State: The Formation of the Patriarchate in Russia], pp. 385–86.
25. Kapterev, *Nikon i Aleksiei,* 2:68–69.
26. Ibid., 2:69–70.
27. Verkhovskoi, *Uchrezhdenie,* 1:39.
28. Ibid., 1:40–41.
29. Ibid., 1:41.
30. Ibid., 1:41, 684.
31. Ibid., 1:42.
32. This term, unless qualified in meaning, is open to differing interpretations. Thus Parker (*Christianity and the State,* p. 126) uses it in reference to: (1) the involvement by ecclesiastical persons and corporations of Western Europe in temporal administration, and (2) the degree to which the authority of the pope was "assimilated in theory to political power." The first of these uses is similar to the meaning that the term has in the present introduction with regard to the performance of judicial-administrative functions by the Russian clergy. The second use is quite the opposite of the meaning given the term in the present introduction. For, with Peter, there was accelerated a movement by the state to impose its secular authority upon the church and direct it in its functions rather than an effort by the church to assume the authority, functions, and prerogatives of the temporal power. In the Petrine period the term "secularization of the church" makes reference to the degree to which the state was successful in assuming authority over the Russian ecclesiastical establishment and in having acknowledged as valid by the ecclesiastical hierarchy the theoretical formulations that polemicists for the state devised in justifying that assumption of authority.
33. The writer is indebted for this point to Professor Georges Florovsky, who spoke on the subject in a lecture at the University of Washington on 29 June 1961 as part of a course on Russian intellectual history.
34. Translation of *Monastyrskii prikaz.*
35. For the text of *Ulozhenie Gosudaria, Tsaria i Velikago Kniazia, Aleksieia Mikhailovicha* [The Code of the Sovereign, Tsar and Grand Prince, Alexis Mikhailovich], see *Polnoe sobranie zakonov,* 1:1–161, no. 1, 29 January 7157/1649.
36. Kapterev, *Nikon i Aleksiei,* 2:125; id., *Patriarkh Nikon i ego protivniki v dielie ispravleniia tserkovnykh obriadov. Vremia patriar-*

shestva Iosifa [Patriarch Nikon and His Opponents in the Correction of Church Rites; the Patriarchate of Joseph]; William Palmer, *The Patriarch and the Tsar;* "Zhitie sviatieishago patriarkha Nikona, pisannoe niekotorym byvshim pri nem klirikom" [The Life of His Eminence, Patriarch Nikon, Written by a Contemporary Cleric], 3:1–110.

37. See the present translation, p. 10.
38. G. Ostrogorsky, *History of the Byzantine State,* pp. 213–14.
39. Kapterev, *Nikon i Aleksiei,* 2:251–52.
40. The Council of 1551. It received the name *Stoglavyi sobor* (The Council of the Hundred Chapters) from the collection of the one hundred chapters (often quite brief) in which were registered its decisions. The name initially applied to it, *Stoglavnik,* by the seventeenth-century scribes who copied that collection became transformed in scholarly works to the form by which it is now known. See "Stoglav," *Entsiklopedicheskii slovar'* [The Encyclopedic Dictionary], pp. 666–68. A number of the practices and observances that Nikon contravened and sought to eradicate had been not merely approved, but explicitly prescribed by the council. Among them: the form for making the sign of the cross, both by the people on their own persons and by the clergy in administering their blessing (chap. 31); the singing of the *Alleluia* twice (chap. 42) instead of three times as demanded by Nikon (*Stoglav* [The Hundred Chapters], pp. 75, 111).
41. Quoted in D. Obolensky, "Russia's Byzantine Heritage," p. 45.
42. Ibid., pp. 45–46.
43. Kapterev, *Nikon i Aleksiei,* 2:538.
44. Ibid., 2:538–39.
45. Ibid., 2:539. For a different view of the significance of the schism, see V. V. Andreev, *Raskol i ego znachenie v narodnoi russkoi istorii* [The Schism and Its Significance in the History of the Russian People].
46. Translation of *miestnichestvo,* a system used for granting appointments to state offices by the grand princes and tsars of the Muscovite state to individuals on the basis of precedence as determined by genealogy and the relative standing of registered families among each other. According to V. O. Kliuchevsky, the elements of *miestnichestvo* began to coalesce into a system in Moscow during the reigns of Ivan III (1462–1505) and his son, Vasilii III (1505–1533); see his *Sochineniia v vos'mi tomakh* [Works in Eight Volumes] (vols. 1–5: *Kurs russkoi istorii* [A Course in Russian History]), 2:153.
47. A. S. Lappo-Danilevsky, "Ideia gosudarstva i glavnieishie momenty eia razvitiia v Rossii so vremeni smuty i do epokhi preobrazovanii" [The Idea of the State and the Most Important Moments of Its Development From the Time of Troubles to the Period of Reforms], quoted in Verkhovskoi, *Uchrezhdenie,* 1:85.
48. Ibid. Lappo-Danilevsky does not specifically make reference to the Counter Reformation.
49. Ibid.

50. M. Karpovich, *Imperial Russia, 1801–19.7*, p. 3.

51. Muscovite secretaries were apparently puzzled at first how to register this ungainly dual title in official records. They initially resorted to the expedient of placing two entirely separate headings, one below the other, on every document issued in the names of the sovereigns, one heading for each of the full titles of the two co-tsars. This, however, proved cumbersome and awkward, and on 26 May 1682 an ukase was issued ordering a halt to the practice (*Polnoe sobranie zakonov*, 2:401–2, no. 921). For the version that was finally authorized, with the title in plural number, see the charter from the co-tsars to Ivan Samoilovich, hetman of the "left-bank" Zaporozhian Cossacks, dated 5 June 1682 (ibid., 2:405–10, no. 927).

52. The Muscovite state had entered this war against the Ottoman Empire in 1686 during the regency of Peter's half-sister Sophia (1682–89). Peter, having inherited this war, tried to put it to his advantage as a means for testing his burgeoning military establishment in engagements on a scale greater than field exercises between his own troops. In 1696, after initial setbacks, Peter's combined land and naval forces succeeded in capturing the Turkish fortified city of Azov, which the Turks formally ceded to the Russians by the treaty of 3 July 1700, the text of which is contained in *Polnoe sobranie zakonov*, 4:66–72, no. 1804. Eleven years later, however, the Turks regained the city.

53. P. N. Miliukov et al., *History of Russia*, 1:177.

54. P. N. Miliukov, *Gosudarstvennoe khoziaistvo Rossii v pervoi chetverti XVIII stoletiia i reforma Petra Velikago* [The State Economy of Russia in the First Quarter of the Eighteenth Century and the Reform of Peter the Great], pp. 175–76; 490–91; 494–95.

55. Detailed reference to the "charter of the Great Sovereign Tsar and Grand Prince," dated 6 December 1695, was made by Afanasii, archbishop of Kholmogory, in his own charter sent to Hegumen Ieremiia of the Veliko-Ustiuzhskii Arkhangel'skii Monastery (*Akty, sobrannye v bibliotekakh i arkhivakh Rossiiskoi imperii Arkheograficheskoiu ekspeditsieiu Imperatorskoi Akademii nauk* [Records Collected in the Libraries and Archives of the Russian Empire by the Archaeographical Expedition of the Imperial Academy of Sciences], 4, no. 315:466–47). See also B. G. Slitsan, "Reforma tserkovnogo upravleniia" [The Reform of the Church Administration], *Ocherki istorii SSSR. Rossiia v pervoi chetverti XVIII v.* [Essays on the History of the USSR; Russia in the First Quarter of the Eighteenth Century], p. 373.

56. *Polnoe sobranie zakonov*, 3:529–30, no. 1664.

57. The phrase is from Runkevich (*Istoria Russkoi Tserkvi*, p. 25), who uses it, however, in reference specifically to two ukases issued only as late as 1698. Previous Petrine ukases that brought the state into church economic affairs Runkevich regards as being fully in accord with precedents established in earlier Muscovite legislation, though he neglects to make definite citations in support of his conclusion.

58. A biographical sketch may be found in *Chteniia v Imperatorskom obshchestvie istorii i drevnostei rossiiskikh* [Readings Before the Imperial Society of History and Russian Antiquities], pp. 29–36.

59. The Saint Nicholas Hermitage Monastery (*Sviato Nikol'sky Pustynnyi monastyr'*), near Kiev, is known to have existed since the seventeenth century. The rank of a hegumen approximates that of an abbot in Roman Catholic monasteries. For a portrayal of Iavorsky's career as *locum tenens,* see J. Šerech, "Stefan Iavorski and the Conflict of Ideologies in the Age of Peter the Great," pp. 40–62. See also the articles entitled "Stefan Iavorsky" by P. E. Shchegolev and A. Korolev in, respectively, (1) *Entsiklopedicheskii slovar',* pp. 538–41 and (2) *Russkii biograficheskii slovar'* [The Russian Biographical Dictionary], pp. 413–22. A biographical study of Iavorsky was made by F. Ternovsky, entitled "M. Stefan Iavorsky" [Metropolitan Stefan Iavorsky], *Trudy Kievskoi dukhovnoi akademii* [Transactions of the Kiev Theological Academy], (January 1864), pp. 36–70; (March), pp. 237–90; (June), pp. 137–86. With regard to the significance of Iavorsky and his antagonist, Feofan Prokopovich, as theologians, ecclesiastical hierarchs, and preachers, the definitive work remains Iu. F. Samarin's *Stefan Iavorskii i Feofan Prokopovich* [Stefan Iavorsky and Feofan Prokopovich].

60. Varlaam Iasinsky, who, before he became metropolitan of Kiev in 1690, was responsible for persuading Iavorsky to enter the monastic life (ibid.).

61. N. M. Nikol'sky, "Tserkovnaia reforma Petra" [Peter's Church Reform], p. 185.

62. By the tsar's personal ukase, dated 24 January 1701. *Polnoe sobranie zakonov,* 4:133, no. 1829. On the beginnings of an articulate policy with respect to the church in the reign of Peter, see Kartashev, *Ocherki,* 2:327–29.

63. Nikol'sky, "Tserkovnaia reforma," p. 188.

64. Ibid., pp. 186–87.

65. Bissonnette, "Pufendorf," pp. 123–29.

66. Verkhovskoi, *Uchrezhdenie,* 1:x–xi, 195.

67. See the present translation, p. 3.

68. See the present translation, p. 6.

69. Schmemann, *The Historical Road,* p. 332.

70. Verkhovskoi, *Uchrezhdenie,* 1:621–60.

71. The term "Most Holy Ruling Synod," or any variation of it employing the word "Synod," was deliberately avoided in the early drafts and in the published version of the *Spiritual Regulation.* Feofan Prokopovich used the word "Synod" several times when he was composing the draft of the *Regulation,* but it was later crossed out and replaced by "Spiritual College," except when used in a general sense; see the present translation, pp. 8–9. Verkhovskoi attributes this to Peter's predilection for the collegial system and his consequent effort to set up a uniform ad-

ministration composed of colleges; *Uchrezhdenie,* 1:498. The names "Most Holy Synod" and "Most Holy Ruling Synod" were authorized, initially for liturgical use, at the meeting of the Spiritual College on 14 February 1721 by a tsarist resolution (*Polnoe sobranie zakonov,* 6:355–56, no. 3734).

72. Verkhovskoi, *Uchrezhdenie,* 1:535–45.

73. The influence of specific individuals in this regard has yet to be ascertained. In speaking about the transformation, Verkhovskoi (ibid., 1:xii) says: "The Spiritual College, as represented in the *Spiritual Regulation,* undoubtedly elicited against itself, even before its opening, a movement by the clergy, which, unable to avoid the inevitable, applied all its efforts to endowing the new institution with a more ecclesiastical appearance and to returning to it at least some of the powers taken away from the church authority during the period of the *locum tenens* and the Central Administration of Monasteries."

74. Ibid., 1: cxlix, clxi–clxii. On an interesting twist to the argument, in which it was claimed that Prokopovich was responsible for creating an organizational imbalance in the Synod to the advantage of the clergy, see Verkhovskoi, *K voprosu o "fal'sifikatsii" Dukhovnago reglamenta* [On the Question of the "Falsification" of the Spiritual Regulation].

75. On the lack of respect shown the Synod by bishops and other clergy, see Verkhovskoi, *Uchrezhdenie,* 1:564.

76. Florovsky, *Puti,* p. 88.

77. *Vysochaishiia rezoliutsii,* literally "supreme resolutions," is customarily translated "imperial resolutions." However, in this case, even though this distinction is not made in Russian, two English terms are employed because some of the resolutions were published before Peter officially became emperor on 22 October 1721; see *Polnoe sobranie zakonov,* 6:444–46, no. 3840. For the resolutions, see ibid., 6:355–56, no. 3734; pp. 371–72, no. 3761; pp. 455–59, no. 3854; and pp. 560–52, no. 3963.

78. Ibid., 6:413–19, no. 3814.

79. Ibid., 6:721–22, no. 4036.

80. See the present translation, p. 6.

81. Florovsky, *Puti,* p. 82.

82. D. A. Zharinov, "Petr Velikii kak zakonodatel' i 'Pravda voli monarshei'" [Peter the Great as Legislator and "The Justice of the Monarch's Will"], p. 163.

83. Kliuchevsky, *Sochineniia,* pp. 61–62.

84. Miliukov, *Gosudarstvennoe khoziaistvo Rossii,* p. 526.

85. Id., *Ocherki po istorii russkoi kul'tury* [Essays on the History of Russian Culture], 3:188.

86. Ibid.

87. Heinrich Fick, a native of Holstein, was admitted to Russian service in 1715 and was sent secretly several times to Sweden to learn

about the system of state administration there. On Fick's influence upon the establishment of the collegial system in Russian state administration, see V. I. Ger'e [Guerrier], *Sbornik pisem i memorialov Leibnitsa otnosiashchikhsia k Rossii i Petru Velikomu* [A Collection of Leibnitz' Letters and Memorials Concerning Russia and Peter the Great], pp. xxii–xxiii. For the text of Fick's report on the Royal Swedish State Chancery, dated 25 April 1718, see Voskresensky, *Zakonodatel'nye akty,* 1:542–49; for the text of the Senate's ukase of 29 November 1721 directing the translation from German into Russian of the regulations and instructions copied and forwarded by Fick, see ibid., 1:95.

88. Miliukov, *Ocherki,* 3:189.

89. In a letter, probably incorrectly attributed to Leibnitz, Peter was told that a state can be made to flourish only by means of establishing good institutions: namely, colleges. For, as with clocks, in which one wheel is brought into movement by contact with others, so in a large state mechanism one college must lead another into movement. Then, if everything is organized in balance and harmony, the hands of life will inevitably point to propitious hours for a state in which the administration is thus arranged. Among the colleges mentioned as being suitable for inclusion is one called *Ein Religions-Collegium.* For the text of this letter, see Ger'e [Guerrier], *Sbornik pisem,* pp. 364–69; for a discussion of it, and on the question of its authorship, see ibid., pp. xx–xxiv.

90. Leibnitz' influence on Peter and his reforms is discussed in Ger'e [Guerrier], *Sbornik pisem,* pp. xii–xxiv, passim; and id., "Otnosheniia Leibnitsa k Petru Velikomu" [Leibnitz' Relations With Peter the Great], 147:1–48, 345–415; 148:309–90. See also E. Iu. Perfetsky, *Car Peter I i Leibnitz* [Tsar Peter I and Leibnitz] and V. Chuchmarev, *G. V. Leibnits i russkaia kul'tura* [G. W. Leibnitz and Russian Culture].

91. From the standpoint of time, Lee was probably the first to direct to Peter a proposal concerning the desirability of his establishing a college for "the propagation of the Christian religion." See Verkhovskoi, *Uchrezhdenie,* 1:145. As Guerrier points out, however, no single person can be assigned the distinction of having furnished Peter with a model for the reform of the state administration along lines sure to be suggested to him by collegial forms already existing in neighboring countries (*Sbornik pisem,* p. xxiv).

92. Marc Szeftel, "Russian Government Before 1905–06," p. 106.

93. Ibid.

94. Zharinov, "Petr Velikii," p. 167.

95. Ibid.

96. V. Ia. Ulanov, *Preobrazovanie upravleniia pri Petrie Velikom* [Administrative Reform Under Peter the Great], p. 221.

97. The growth of Russia's military prowess under Peter is alluded to even in the *Spiritual Regulation;* see the present translation, p. 30.

98. Voskresensky, *Zakonodatel'nye akty*, 1:115. Peter's ukase, undated, is assigned to the beginning of January, 1722.
99. M. M. Bogoslovsky, "Petr Velikii" [Peter the Great], pp. 28–30. See also Zharinov, "Petr Velikii," pp. 156–67.
100. Bogoslovsky, "Petr Velikii," p. 28.
101. Pp. xiii ff., supra.
102. Kapterev, *Nikon i Aleksiei*, 2:50–121.
103. M. D'iakonov, *Vlast' moskovskikh gosudarei. Ocherki iz istorii politicheskikh idei drevnei Rusi do kontsa XVI vieka* [The Authority of the Muscovite Sovereigns; Essays on the Political Ideas of Early Rus' to the End of the Sixteenth Century], p. 85.
104. Kartashev, *Ocherki*, 2:341.
105. See the present translation, p. 8.
106. Kartashev, *Ocherki*, 2:341.
107. See the present translation, pp. 34–35.
108. See the present translation, pp. 13–20, 43, 58, 62–63.
109. Florovsky, *Puti*, pp. 83–84.
110. See the present translation, pp. 50–62.
111. *Polnoe sobranie zakonov*, 6:128–29, no. 3515, 10 February 1720.
112. Ibid., 4:360–62, no. 2130, 30 December 1706; p. 375, no. 2142, 17 March 1707; p. 383, no. 2154, 25 July 1707; p. 393, no. 2166, 31 October 1707; p. 401, no. 2185, 15 January 1708; p. 483, no. 2263, 13 March 1710; pp. 761–63, no. 2454, 27 November 1711.
113. Ibid., 4:11, no. 1757, 14 February 1700; p. 192, no. 1908, 14 February 1702; p. 308, no. 2054, 30 May 1705; 5:554–55, no. 3183, 16 March 1718.
114. Ibid., 4:401, no. 2186, 15 January 1710; p. 581, no. 2308, 11 November 1710; 5:78, no. 2762, 20 January 1714; p. 86, no. 2778, 27 February 1714; pp. 751–52, no. 3447, 6 November 1719; 6:187–88, no. 3575, 30 April 1720; p. 358, no. 3741, 16 February 1721; p. 455, no. 3854, 19 November 1721 (art. 10); pp. 697–99, no. 4021, 31 May 1722; p. 781, no. 4105, 8 October 1722; pp. 792–94, no. 4126, 30 November 1722.
115. Ibid., 6:188–89, no. 3576, 3 May 1720.
116. Ibid., 6:399, no. 2179, 19 December 1707.
117. See the present translation, pp. 81–82.
118. *Polnoe sobranie zakonov*, 4:431–32, no. 2213, 12 November 1708. The solemn ceremony of anathematization referred to in this ukase was directed against Hetman Ivan Mazepa, whose change of support in favor of Charles XII of Sweden at a critical time in the Northern War Peter could not forgive. The sermon at that ceremony was delivered by Stefan Iavorsky. It has been published under the title "Slovo pred prokliatiem Mazepy, proiznesennoe mitropolitom Stefanom Iavorskim v Moskovskom Uspenskom soborie, 12 noiabria 1708 g." [The

Sermon at the Anathematization of Mazepa, Given by Metropolitan Stefan Iavorsky in the Assumption Cathedral in Moscow on 12 November 1708], pp. 499–512.

119. Mark Pattison, *Essays*, 2:45–55.

120. Thomas Hobbes, *Leviathan*, p. 86.

121. Bogoslovsky, "Petr Velikii," p. 29.

122. Ibid., pp. 30–33; Zharinov, "Petr Velikii," p. 167.

123. Florovsky, *Puti*, p. 85.

124. Kliuchevsky, *Sochineniia*, 4:47.

125. Sumner, *Peter the Great*, p. 20. On the events of this period, especially those of 15 May 1682, see S. M. Soloviev, *Istoriia Rossii s drevneishikh vremen* [The History of Russia From the Earliest Times], 7:270–73; Bogoslovsky, "Petr Velikii," p. 16; id., "Dietstvo Petra Velikago" [Peter the Great's Childhood], 5–29.

126. Kliuchevsky, *Sochineniia*, 4:10.

127. Ibid., 4:9.

128. It was in the German suburb that Peter may first have become acquainted with the collegial system generally and in particular as it pertained to ecclesiastical administration (Verkhovskoi, *Uchrezhdenie*, 1:71; Kartashev, *Ocherki*, 2:324).

129. Verkhovskoi, *Uchrezhdenie*, 1:72–77; he mentions (ibid., 1:74–76) that Peter on his visit to England was on one occasion received as the guest of King George. He cites as his reference I. Golikov, *Dieianiia Petra Velikago* [The Deeds of Peter the Great], 1:126–27. Kartashev (*Ocherki*, 2:324), without indicating a reference, repeats that detail. This, of course, is an anachronism. Golikov (*Dieianiia*, 1:126) correctly states that Peter's visitor was *Korol' Vel'gel'm*, who would have been William III (1689–1702). On the other hand, the "King George" referred to by the aforementioned authors was in reality Prince George of Denmark, whom Peter met when he returned the king's visit several days later early in 1698. George, brother of Danish King Christian V, was the husband of Princess Anne, who reigned as queen of England from 1702 to 1714. He died in 1708 (Bogoslovsky, *Petr I. Materialy dlia biografii* [Peter I; Materials for a Biography], 4:301, 589).

130. *Polnoe sobranie zakonov*, 6:650, no. 3963, 12 April 1722. Article 15 of these imperial resolutions granted authority in such matters to the Synod. For the text of the Synod's request for verification of other parts of these resolutions, see Voskresensky, *Zakonodatel'nye akty*, 1:103.

131. Kliuchevsky, *Sochineniia*, 4:19.

132. Soloviev, *Istoriia Rossii*, 7:449, 574–75.

133. Verkhovskoi, *Uchrezhdenie*, 1:69–71.

134. Karpovich, *Imperial Russia*, p. 8.

135. "Feofan Prokopovich," *Entsiklopedicheskii slovar'*, pp. 929–30; B. Titlinov, "Feofan Prokopovich," *Russkii biograficheskii slovar'* [The Russian Biographical Dictionary], 25:399–448; for an as-

sessment of Prokopovich's literary activity, see P. Morozov, "Feofan Prokopovich kak pisatel'" [Feofan Prokopovich as a Writer], *Zhurnal
Ministerstva narodnago prosvieshcheniia* [The Journal of the Ministry
of Public Education], (February 1880), pp. 416–75; (March 1880),
pp. 72–133; (May–June 1880), pp 107–48, 251–311;
(July–August 1880), pp. 1–49, 293–354; (September 1880), pp.
1–65; N. Barsov, "Lichnost' Feofana Prokopovicha" [The Personality
of Feofan Prokopovich], *Istoricheskie, kriticheskie i polemicheskie opyty*
[Historical, Critical, and Polemical Studies], pp. 114–27; Samarin,
Stefan i Feofan; I. A. Chistovich, *Feofan Prokopovich i ego vremia*
[Feofan Prokopovich and His Time]; A. N. Pypin, "Feofan Prokopovich
i ego protivniki" [Feofan Prokopovich and His Opponents], pp.
791–818; F. Venturi, "Feofan Prokopovič," pp. 625–80.

136. According to Verkhovskoi this occurred probably at about the
same time that Peter, in a tsarist resolution dated 20 November 1718,
first publicly alluded to the possibility of his establishing the Spiritual
College; (*Uchrezhdenie,* 1:156, 203). For the text of the resolution, see
Polnoe sobranie zakonov, 5:594–95, no. 3239; for an English translation of it, see Bissonnette, "Pufendorf," p. 21.

137. The origins of the Kiev Academy, from whose halls emerged
generations of scholars with a pervasive and fructifying influence on
Russian culture and religious life, go back directly to 1631. In that year,
Peter Mogila, acting in his capacity as great archimandrite (*velikii ar-
khimandrit*) of the Kiev Monastery of the Caves, a post that made him
independent of the metropolitan of Kiev and placed him nominally
under the immediate jurisdiction of the patriarch of Constantinople,
founded a school of higher learning at the monastery "for the teaching
of the liberal arts in Greek, Slavonic, and Latin." In the following year
Mogila himself became metropolitan of Kiev and he joined his school
with that which had been organized and run since 1615 by the Kiev
Brotherhood. The combination of these two schools gave rise to the institution that came to incorporate in its title the name of its founder, the
Kiev-Mogila College.

There is disagreement among historians over the time that this college became the Kiev Academy. D. Vishnevsky, a specialist on the history of the Kiev Academy, considers 11 January 1694 to be significant
in this regard, because on that date a tsarist charter granted to the
Kiev-Mogila College an expanded curriculum (to include theology), internal administrative autonomy, and jurisdiction over its students (*Kievskaia akademiia v pervoi polovinie XVIII stoletiia* [The Kiev Academy
in the First Half of the Eighteenth Century], pp. 3–4). Vishnevsky
further holds, as do other authorities on the Kiev Academy, that a subsequent charter, issued by Peter on 26 September 1701, in addition to
confirming the rights bestowed by the 1694 charter, formally authorized
an actual change of designation from "college" to "academy." This latter
point, however, is contested by K. V. Kharlampovich, who observes that

the term "academy" was used in the 1701 charter only in explanation of the grounds for the issuance of the charter and not in any formal act of redesignation (*Malorossiiskoe vliianie na velikorusskuiu tserkovnuiu zhizn'* [Little Russian Influence on Great Russian Church Life], 1:411). Indeed, the Kiev-Mogila College does not appear to have been officially called an "academy" for many years after the granting of the 1701 charter. As late as 1742, in a confirmatory charter issued on 11 December by Empress Elizabeth, it was still not referred to by that name (ibid.). Contemporary Russian usage recognized such diverse designations (referring to it in plural number) as: *bratskiia shkoly* (fraternal schools) and *uchilishcha* (institutes of higher learning) (ibid., p. 410). Still, Kharlampovich agrees with Vishnevsky in saying that, for the reasons cited above, the college from 1694 onwards *could have been* properly referred to as an "academy," even though contemporaries more often than not refrained from doing so. Accordingly the more familiar name, Kiev Academy, is adhered to in the present work.

138. Verkhovskoi, *Uchrezhdenie,* 1:119–21, lists the scholarly books in Prokopovich's library that he considers pertinent to an understanding of the sources of the *Spiritual Regulation.* He also (ibid., 2, pt. 5:3–71) furnishes a historical sketch of the library, its complete inventory, and an onomastic index.

139. Morozov, "Feofan Prokopovich kak pisatel," (June 1880), p. 297. Prokopovich's own views are expressed in "Vyderzhki iz rukopisnoi retoriki F. Prokopovicha, soderzhashchiia v sebie izobrazhenie papistov i iezuitov" [Extracts From the Written Rhetoric of F. Prokopovich, Containing a Depiction of Papists and Jesuits], pp. 614–37. For the relationship between Prokopovich and Buddeus, see R. Stupperich, "Feofan Prokopovič und Johann Buddeus," pp. 341–62.

140. Translation and abridgement of *O pravdie voli monarshei v opredielenie svoikh po sebie nasliednikov* [On the Justice of the Monarch's Will in His Own Determination of His Heirs]. This was the title given the document by its author, Feofan Prokopovich, in his report to Peter, dated 24 August 1722. See Voskresensky, *Zakonodatel'nye akty,* 1:113–14. *The Justice of the Monarch's Will* formed the basis for the Ustav [Statute] of 5 February 1722 on succession to the throne (*Polnoe sobranie zakonov,* 6:496–97, no. 3893). Peter commissioned Prokopovich to write the *Justice of the Monarch's Will* in vindication and support of his decision to remove as heir to the throne his son Alexis in favor of the latter's infant half brother, Peter. This decision was announced in the Manifesto of 3 February 1718 (*Polnoe sobranie zakonov,* 5:534–39, no. 3151); also contained in Voskresensky, *Zakonodatel'nye akty,* 1:164–69.

141. Verkhovskoi, *Uchrezhdenie,* 1:126.

142. Verkhovskoi concludes (ibid., 1:87) that the views expressed in the *Justice of the Monarch's Will* represent those held by Prokopovich alone and not shared in all respects by Peter, as claimed by Lappo-Dani-

levsky. In Prokopovich's view, says Verkhovskoi, the source of the monarch's authority is the people, while Peter considered himself to exercise authority by the grace of God. Nevertheless the different concepts of the origin of the monarch's authority, although they remained unreconciled, did not in this case lead to different views concerning the application of that authority, since in both cases it was regarded as being absolute.

143. See, for example, the present translation, p. 11. Peter regarded the pacifist values engendered by the church and the depletion by it of the state's economic and human resources as debilitating the material safety and well-being of the state, such debilitation having proved fatal in the case of the Byzantine Empire (*Polnoe sobranie zakonov,* vol. 5, no. 3264 and vol. 6, no. 3840). His attitude can further be discerned in the objects of derision chosen for masquerades, festivals, and such mock institutions as the "Most Mad, All-Frolicsome, and All-Drunken Council," which meticulously avoided caricaturing Protestant personages, rites, or institutions while heaping ribald ridicule upon those that were Roman Catholic or Orthodox. For a sampling of various interpretations with regard to the purposes, if any besides mere entertainment, that Peter may have had in mind in staging these farces, see Golikov, *Dieianiia,* 5:592–93 and 6:277–90; Kliuchevsky, *Sochineniia,* 4: 39–42; "Shutki i potiekhi Petra Velikago: sobstvennoruchno im napisannye chiny izbraniia i postavleniia kniaz'papy, shutochnyia poslaniia, ukazy, rospisi i podpiski 1690–1725 gg." [Peter the Great's Jokes and Games: the Rites of Election and Installation of the Prince-Pope, Jocose Letters, Ukases, Assignments, and Signatures Written in His Own Hand, 1690–1725], pp. 845–92; I. Nosovich, "Vsep'ianieishii sobor, uchrezhdennyi Petrom Velikim" [The All-Drunken Council Established by Peter the Great], pp. 734–39. See also F. Ternovsky, "Imperator Petr I-i v ego otnosheniiakh k katolichestvu i protestantstvu" [Emperor Peter I in His Relations With Catholicism and Protestantism], pp. 373–404.

144. Verkhovskoi, *Uchrezhdenie,* 1:303–11.

145. Ibid., 1:289–93.

146. Ibid., 1:310.

147. Ibid., 1:268.

148. Ibid., 1:123, 312.

149. Bissonnette, "Pufendorf," pp. 3, 41.

150. Ibid., p. 325.

151. Verkhovskoi, *Uchrezhdenie,* 1:90–91.

152. See the present translation, p. 37.

153. Pr. Smith, *Origins of Modern Culture, 1543–1684,* p. 216.

154. Verkhovskoi, *Uchrezhdenie,* 1:301–2.

155. Florovsky, *Puti,* p. 87.

156. Verkhovskoi, *Uchrezhdenie,* 1:273.

157. Ibid.; 1:141. For the text of the letter translated into Russian, see "Materialy dlia istorii russkoi religioznoi i tserkovnoi zhizni. (Pis'ma

Feofana Prokopovicha.) Pis'mo k Iakovu Markovichu—iz Peterburga ot 10 maia 1720 g." [Materials for the History of Russian Religious and Ecclesiastical Life. (The Letters of Feofan Prokopovich.)], pp. 287–94.

158. Verkhovskoi, *Uchrezhdenie*, 1:262–63.
159. Pp. xxviii–xxix supra.
160. Verkhovskoi, *Uchrezhdenie*, 1:263.
161. Ibid., 1:263–64.
162. Schmemann, *The Historical Road*, p. 333.
163. Ibid.
164. Samarin, *Stefan i Feofan*, p. 252.
165. Florovsky, *Puti*, p. 84.

Translation

1. The original fair draft of the Manifesto contains, beneath a small cross at the top (which P. V. Verkhovskoi interprets as being used to invoke a blessing upon the subsequent written labors), the following heading: "We, Peter the First, Tsar and Autocrat of All-Russia, Etc., Etc., Etc." At the end of the document, located on the lower right-hand side, there is the signature "Peter," while the place and date of signing are on the lower left-hand side, "In Petersburg, on the 25th of January 1721" (P. V. Verkhovskoi, *Uchrezhdenie Dukhovnoi kollegii i Dukhovnyi reglament. K voprosu ob otnoshenii Tserkvi i gosudarstva v Rossii* [The Establishment of the Spiritual College and the Spiritual Regulation; On the Question of the Relations of Church and State in Russia], 2, pt. 1:3–4 (hereafter, *Uchrezhenie*); V. N. Beneshevich, *Sbornik pamiatnikov po istorii tserkovnago prava, preimushchestvenno Russkoi Tserkvi do epokhi Petra Velikago* [A Collection of Monuments on the History of Ecclesiastical Law, Principally of the Russian Church to the Period of Peter the Great], 2:90).

2. Césaire Tondini suggests that, in alluding to the "kings of the New Testament" (those of the Christian dispensation), Prokopovich may have had in mind the Roman emperor Constantine the Great, among others (*Règlement ecclésiastique de Pierre le Grand*, p. 2). To Verkhovskoi the primary characteristic of this passage is its ambiguity. This, he believes, reflects the vexing problem faced by Prokopovich, and never resolved satisfactorily, in vindicating through historical example the assertion of rights over purely ecclesiastical matters by the state under Peter (*Uchrezhdenie*, 1:282–83).

3. The clause in parentheses was added by Peter personally in the edited, or foul, draft of the *Spiritual Regulation* (ibid., 2, pt. 1:6). For a description of the four extant MSS of the *Spiritual Regulation* (Prokopovich's original rough draft is not among them), see ibid., 2, pt. 1:12–25.

4. The final paragraph of the Manifesto is Peter's, added in his own handwriting in the edited draft (ibid., 2, pt. 1:⁷).

5. Eleven signatures follow at this point in the oath. That such an oath be signed by incoming members of the Spiritual College was decreed in the last sentence of the Manifesto, which Peter himself wrote into that document. Earlier, it had been his intention that the members of all the newly established secular colleges, when entering upon their duties, execute a standard oath, which appeared as a part of the *General'nyi reglament* [The General Regulation], dated 28 February 1720 (for the text of the oath, see *Polnoe sobranie zakonov Rossiiskoi imperii s 1649 goda* [The Complete Collection of the Laws of the Russian Empire from 1649], 6:146, no. 3534 and N. A. Voskresensky, ed., *Zakonodatel'nye akty Petra I* [The Legislative Acts of Peter I], pp. 483–84, with variants on pp. 414–15, 454, 463, 468; on the expression of Peter's desire for state functionaries to take this oath, see his ukase of 19 June 1719 in ibid., pp. 72–73). This standard oath for state functionaries, left essentially intact but with modified language and additional detail to make it suitable for application in an ecclesiastical context, was then used as the model for the oath to be given the incoming members of the Spiritual College (Verkhovskoi, *Uchrezhdenie*, 1: 188–89; 2, pt. 1:9).

The fair draft of the oath, to which the clergymen listed below affixed their signatures, became its final recension, fully reproduced thereafter with only minor typographical alterations in all printed editions, until the oath's abrogation on 23 February 1901 (ibid., 1:189–90; 2:9).

At its inception the organization of the Spiritual College followed the arrangement stipulated for it in the Manifesto of 25 January 1721: one president, two vice-presidents, four councilors, and four assessors. These offices were supposed to be filled by persons whose ecclesiastical ranks accorded with those specified in part 3, article 1 of the *Spiritual Regulation* (q.v.): bishops, archimandrites, hegumens, and archpriests. In keeping with these requirements, the president and two vice-presidents were chosen from men of episcopal rank (one metropolitan and two archbishops) and the four councilors were all archimandrites. Of the four assessors, however, only one, a protopresbyter, was qualified by rank. The remaining three consisted of an hieromonk and two priests, of whom one was Greek. Rapid promotions of the latter three assessors, however, put the matter in order within little over a year.

Prokopovich, it may be noted, signed this oath as "archbishop of Pskov" whereas in the preceding year he had signed the *Spiritual Regulation* as "bishop" of that same see. He had been elevated on 31 December 1720 at Peter's personal intervention to the rank of archbishop, even though in 1717, in line with the tsar's general policy of eliminating metropolias as they became vacant through natural attrition, the former metropolia of Pskov had been reduced in status not to an archbishopric but a bishopric (N. Ustrialov, *Istoriia tsarstvovaniia Petra Velikago* [History of the Reign of Peter the Great], 4, pt. 1:551).

On 27 January 1721, then, the following clergymen subscribed to this oath as shown below (their signatures appearing in a single column, one beneath the other). On 9 February they held a preliminary session at the hospice of the Alexander Nevsky Monastery in Saint Petersburg in preparation for their first formal meeting five days later, at which, as mentioned in the introduction, the name "Spiritual College" was discarded in favor of "Most Holy Ruling Synod" (T. Barsov, *Sviatieishii sinod v ego proshlom* [The Most Holy Synod in Its Past], pp. 201–2).

Humble Stefan [Iavorsky], Metropolitan of Riazan'; Feodosii [Ianovsky], Archbishop of Novgorod and Archimandrite of the Alexander Nevsky [Monastery in Saint Petersburg]; Feofan [Prokopovich], Archbishop of Pskov; Gavriil [Buzhinsky], Archimandrite of the [Moscow] Ipatsky Trinity Monastery; Peter [Smielich], Archimandrite of the [Moscow] Simonov Monastery; Leonid, Archimandrite of the Petrovsky [Monastery in Rostov]; Ierofei [Prilutsky], Archimandrite of the [Moscow] Donskoi Monastery; Priest Anastasios Kontoeidēs; Protopresbyter Ioann Simeonov of the Trinity [Cathedral in Saint Petersburg]; Priest Peter Grigor'ev of the Sampsonov [Church in Moscow]; Hieromonk Varlaam Osvianikov.

6. The following title was inserted between the first and second sheets of the edited draft (a virgule indicates the end of a line): "By the Grace and Mercy : Of Our Most Loving God/ By the Endeavor and Command/ Of Our God-Given and God-Inspired/ Sovereign and Grand Prince/ PETER THE FIRST/ Autocrat/ Of all Great and Little and White Russia/ etc.: etc.: etc.:/ And by His Consent/ Is Established in the Holy Orthodox Russian Church/ A Spiritual Sanhedrin or College/ That Is/ A Conciliar/ ADMINISTRATION/ of Spiritual Affairs/ With the Concurrence and Decision/ Of the Holy Council and the Ruling Senate/ In the Capital City/ Saint Petersburg/ In the Year 1720 from the Birth of Christ/ The Month of February" (Verkhovskoi, *Uchrezhdenie,* 2, pt. 1:26).

7. In place of the preceding title and the first part of this sentence, the edited draft originally read: "This book, Which Contains a Description of and a Treatise on the Spiritual College, Is Divided Into Three Parts, corresponding. . . ." These words were crossed out and a piece of paper with the present text in Prokopovich's handwriting was pasted over them (ibid., 2, pt. 1:27); see also note 1 of the present introduction.

8. The initial ukase for the formation of colleges was issued on 11 December 1717, in accordance with which the soon-to-be appointed presidents of those colleges were directed to organize them during the following year and prepare them to commence administrative functioning by 1719 (*Polnoe sobranie zakonov,* 5:525, no. 3129). On 16 Decem-

ber 1717 another ukase was issued concerning the appointment of presidents and vice-presidents to nine colleges: *Inostrannykh diel* (Foreign Affairs), *Kamer* (Exchequer), *Iustits* (Justice), *Revezion* (usually spelled *Revizion*) (Accounting), *Voinskaia* (Military), *Admiralteiskaia* (Admiralty), *Kommerts* (Commerce), *Shtats-Kantor* (Comptroller), and *Berg i Manufaktur* (Mines and Manufactures) *Kollegiia* (ibid., 5:527–28, no. 3133). Inertia and a number of delays, exasperating to Peter, beset the actual organization of these colleges, so that while some began functioning in 1719, others failed to start until 1720.

9. Tondini attributes this saying to Euripides (*Règlement ecclésiastique*, p. 18).

10. Prokopovich may have had in mind the passage, directed to the presbyters of Christian communities in Asia Minor, in 1 Peter 5:3: "nor yet as lording it over your charges, but becoming from the heart a pattern to the flock" (ibid., p. 21).

11. Refers to the secular, or married, clergy (ibid., p. 23).

12. Literally, "Educational institutions, and the teachers and students therein, as well as church preachers."

13. Translation of *akafisty,* laudatory chants performed while standing (hence the name from the Greek *akathistos,* "not seated") in honor of the Lord Jesus Christ, the Mother of God, and various saints. Lengthy collections of *akafisty* were published in Kiev and Mogilev, especially in the last decade of the seventeenth century and the beginning of the eighteenth. Among them was one dedicated to the "Tomb of Our Lord and His Resurrection." Verkhovskoi conjectures that it may have been this *akafist* that in the *Spiritual Regulation* was considered "unseemly" on the basis that the church rejoices at the Resurrection of Christ and does not hold penitential services (*Uchrezhdenie,* 1:373).

14. Translation of *sluzhby.*

15. Translation of *molebny.*

16. The fame attaching to Euphrosinus (Evfrosin) of Pskov (1386–1481) influenced the development of the controversy over the proper rendering of the *Alleluia* in prayer. He is supposed to have gone to Joseph, patriarch of Constantinople, in order to seek a decision with regard to that question and to have obtained from the latter an injunction to execute it in double form. This manner of singing *Alleluia* had become prevalent among the people of Pskov, possibly as the result of ritualistic forms emanating from Serbia; and it was to the Pskovians that Metropolitan Photius in 1419 directed an epistle, exhorting them as follows: "And as for the *Alleluia* in the doxology, do you voice it thus: 'Glory to the Father, the Son, and the Holy Ghost, now, and ever, and unto the ages of ages. Amen. Alleluia, alleluia, alleluia, Glory to Thee, O God. Alleluia, alleluia, alleluia, Glory to Thee, O God. Alleluia, alleluia, alleluia, Glory to Thee, O God.'" This is the form observed in the Russian Church at the present time; see Isabel Hapgood, ed., *Service Book of the Holy Orthodox-Catholic Apostolic Church,*

pp. 513, 566. The *Life* of Euphrosinus of Pskov acquired significance in the controversy when, during the Council of the Hundred Chapters (see note 40 of the Introduction), it was used in substantiating the validity of the double *Alleluia* (Verkhovskoi, *Uchrezhdenie,* 1:374–75).

17. Sabellius, a Christian priest active in the second quarter of the third century, propounded teachings that concerned the relationship between the Father and the Son (J. Chapman, "Monarchians," *The Catholic Encyclopedia,* 10:448–51).

18. Nestorius, patriarch of Constantinople from 428 to 431, objected to implications that could be derived from the use of the Greek word *Theotokos,* meaning "Mother of God." To some among the faithful his objection appeared to be insulting to the divinity of the Redeemer, if not actually denying that divinity. The word at whose use he demurred was subsequently entered into the body of prescribed ecclesiastical terminology by the Fifth Ecumenical Council at Constantinople in 553 (J. Chapman, "Nestorius," *The Catholic Encyclopedia,* 10:755–59; A. A. Vasiliev, *History of the Byzantine Empire,* 1:98–99; Henri Grégoire, "The Byzantine Church," *Byzantium,* pp. 95–96; H. R. Percival, *The Seven Ecumenical Councils of the Undivided Church,* p. 313).

19. Special reverence has long been accorded Friday in Christian thought and practice as the day of Christ's Passion. In Russia the honor due Friday (*Piatnitsa*), as a day of the week was frequently combined with veneration of Saint Paraskeva, whose name in Greek, from *paraskeue,* corresponds to *Piatnitsa.* Among the people Saint Paraskeva–Piatnitsa was thought to be the personification of the day, *Piatnitsa.* Thus *Piatnitsa* could wander about the world, making sure of the proper observance of Friday and punishing those who disregarded the prohibitions imposed upon them for that day by delivering them to excruciatingly difficult labors. A. Komarovsky notes that in ancient Rome similar associations existed with regard to Friday as a day dedicated to Venus (*Dies Veneris*), and that those associations later colored Christian practices in Italy, Spain, France, Germany, and elsewhere ("Piatnitsa," *Entsiklopedicheskii slovar'* [The Encyclopedic Dictionary], 50:944–45). Thomas Consett, chaplain of the English Factory, or trading settlement, in Moscow in the time of Peter I, thought that *Piatnitsa* "seems to be the same with Venus of the Heathen, and antiently worship'd by the Russians" (*The Present State and Regulations of the Church in Russia,* 1:26; see also Verkhovskoi, *Uchrezhdenie,* 1:376–78).

20. The practice of fasting on twelve designated, or named, Fridays (*imennyia piatnitsy*) was, according to Verkhovskoi, not unknown in Russia even in 1916. It was apparently based on precepts advocating such fasting contained in the apocryphal *Instruction of Our Father, Saint Clement, Pope of Rome, on the Twelve Fridays.* Verkhovskoi gives the text of this document in *Uchrezhdenie,* 1:377.

21. The *prosfory* (altar-breads; singular, *prosfora*) used in the Divine Liturgy on the feast of the Annunciation of the Birth-Giver of God, 25 March (7 April by the Gregorian calendar), were by Russian peasants thought to possess miraculous properties conducive to producing abundant harvests. Crumbs from these altar-breads were mixed with seed before sowing and with the feed of livestock. During the celebration of Easter matins, peasant women would watch their livestock for certain signs. If the animals remained quiet while the service was in progress, they would, it was thought, prove to be profitable; should they be restless, however, then no good could be expected from them (ibid., 1:379).

22. This view was contained in the *Skazaniia Simona, episkopa Vladimer'skago i Suzhdal'skago o sviatykh chernoriztsekh Pecher'skykh* [The Narratives of Simon, Bishop of Vladimir and Suzdal', on the Holy Monks of the Caves] (ibid.).

23. Translation of *Starodubsky polk,* literally, 'the Starodub Regiment." A *polk* was a military unit and an administrative-territorial district in the Ukraine from the sixteenth to the eighteenth century. This particular *polk,* comprising the city of Starodub itself (located eighty miles southwest of Briansk) and its surrounding towns, was capable of putting into the field a regiment of from six to seven thousand men ("Starodub," *Bol'shaia sovetskaia entsiklopediia,* 2d ed., 40:507; "Polk," ibid., 33:598–99; Consett, *The Present State,* 1:27).

24. These views are still maintained by some. Thus A. Dunn writes, "In 557 Pelagius I caused the tomb [in the church of St. Lawrence-Without-the-Walls in Rome] to be opened for the reception of the body of St. Stephen, the first martyr, which had been transferred from Constantinople." J. Morris, on the other hand, states that the body of St. Stephen lies in a church of Venice. Other traditions have placed the body of St. Stephen in Gaul, Naples, Capua, and elsewhere (A. Dunn [Weedon], *A Pilgrim's Guide to Rome,* pp. 115–16; J. Morris, *The World of Venice,* p. 225; R. Sinker, "Stephen, St.,' *A Dictionary of Christian Antiquities,* 2:1929–33).

25. The reference is to Supplementary Article 6 of the Bishops' Oath of 1716, in which bishops promised to watch ". . . that they do not worship holy icons or invest false miracles for [the people], wherefore cause is given to enemies for casting aspersions upon Orthodox believers, but that they reverence the Holy Orthodox Catholic Church according to reason." For the text of the Oath, see Verkhovskoi, *Uchrezhdenie,* 2, pt. 2: B.

26. The practice of conducting church services in several parts simultaneously was apparently occasioned by the conjunction of three factors. (1) The rites of the Orthodox church developed largely by way of rubrics formulated and observed in monasteries, where their performance proceeds continuously throughout day and night. (2) That vast structure of ritual was ill suited for parish churches, whose needs did not in all respects accord with a strict interpretation of the monastic maxim, *ora et*

labora. (3) There existed a requirement that all church services, whether in monasteries or elsewhere, be performed *in toto,* without curtailment or change. Hence, while in parish churches all parts of the services were indeed performed, the practice arose of combining several of them together for the sake of brevity. The clergy in Muscovite Rus' appeared to realize that there were advantages connected with such foreshortening. Parish priests resorted to this expedient with regularity, while their bishops at times lent it at least tacit approval by refusing to oppose it. The initiative in the efforts to eliminate *dvoeglasie* (chanting in two parts) and *mnogoglasie* (chanting in many parts) lay with the secular authority. Ivan IV brought the matter up before the Council of the Hundred Chapters, and the issue was vigorously pursued by Tsar Alexis (ibid., 1:382; S. M. Soloviev, *Istoriia Rossii s drevneishikh vremen* [The History of Russia from the Earliest Times], 6:203–4; "Patriarkh Nikon po vnov' otkrytym N. A. Gibbenet materialam" [Patriarch Nikon in the Light of Material Recently Uncovered by N. A. Gibbenet], pp. 223–24).

27. 2 Timothy 3:16–17.

28. *The Orthodox Confession of Faith* (in Greek, *Orthodoxos Homologia*) is generally attributed to Peter Mogila, metropolitan of Kiev from 1632 to 1647. According to Verkhovskoi, it was probably compiled at his instance by Isaiah Trofimovich Kozlovsky, hegumen at the Nikol'sky Monastery. It was presented by Mogila to a church council in Kiev in 1640 and was examined by a second council, in Jassy, two years later, which approved it for use as a catechism (*Uchrezhdenie,* 1:387; Tondini, *Règlement ecclésiastique,* p. 48; "Petr Mogila" [Peter Mogila], *Entsiklopedicheskii slovar',* 41:484–85); for the text of the *Orthodox Confession of Faith,* see Antoine Malvy and Marcel Viller, eds., "La Confession Orthodoxe de Pierre Mogila," *Orientalia Christiana,* vol. 10, no. 39.

29. Saint John Chrysostom (345–407), patriarch of Constantinople (C. Baur, "John Chrysostom," *The Catholic Encyclopedia,* 8:452–57; for his works, see Jacques Migne, *Patrologiae cursus completus, series graeca,* vols. 47–64, and F. Dübner, ed., *Sancti Joannis Chrysostomi Opera Selecta*).

30. Theophylact, archbishop of Ochrida in the second half of the eleventh and the beginning of the twelfth century (B. Pashchenko, "Feofilakt" [Theophylact], *Entsiklopedicheskii slovar',* 82:932; for his works, see Migne, *Patrologiae cursus completus, series graeca,* vols. 123–26).

31. In the cited draft, this paragraph ended with the words: ". . . this is to be done lest anyone fancy that we introduce this teaching by ourselves, forsaking the teaching of the holy fathers" (Verkhovskoi, *Uchrezhdenie,* 2, pt. 1; 38).

32. None of the three booklets appeared in Peter's lifetime. Feofan Prokopovich himself made several attempts at writing catechisms. It was not until 1765, however, that there appeared the *Pravoslavnoe uchenie*

[Orthodox Instruction] by Platon, metropolitan of Moscow, which was subsequently recognized by the Synod as satisfying the requirements by which it could be accepted as the first of the three booklets. To take the place of the third booklet, there appeared in 1780 a collection by Gabriel (Gavriil), metropolitan of Novgorod, entitled *Kratkiia poucheniia iz raznykh sv. otets i uchitelei* [Short Precepts From Various Holy Fathers and Doctors]. Finally, in 1787, there was issued the *Nastavlenie o sobstvennykh vsiakago khristianina dolzhnostiakh* [An Instruction on Every Christian's Personal Duties] by Tikhon, bishop of Voronezh, which was approved by the Synod as the second booklet of the trilogy ordered in the *Spiritual Regulation*. None of these three, Verkhovskoi points out, possessed the characteristic of brevity called for in the *Regulation* and none enjoyed widespread popular appeal (*Uchrezhdenie,* 1:386–96).

33. Translation of *klikushi*. A. Ianovsky describes them as women who are subject to hysterical seizures, during which they emit frenzied screams ("Klikushi," *Entsiklopedicheskii slovar',* 29:374–75). Apparently the term had broader application in Peter's time, for his personal ukase of 7 May 1715 refers to both male and female *klikushi,* and contains allusions to the willful pretense of such symptoms (*Polnoe sobranie zakonov,* 5:156–57, no. 2906). It is in this latter vein that Consett, who first translated the term as "Squawlers," described them as "Persons that feign themselves bewitch'd, screeming and shrieking with the utmost Distraction, to move the Compassion of Spectators to give them Money; two or three of these Vagabonds were severely whip'd, and their Imposture detected by the late Emperor in Mosco, 1720" (*The Present State,* 1:38). Some of the symptoms manifested by the *klikushi* and the reaffirmation, under Empress Anne, of Peter's ukase of 1715 concerning them are described by I. S. Bieliaev, "Ikotniki i klikushki" [Hiccoughers and Squawlers], pp. 144–63.

34. Consett offers the following explanation: ". . . this refers to the mistakes of some charitable Persons, who commiserating the Circumstances of such as have not wherewithal to bury their Dead, are often impos'd upon, and told of the Deaths of Persons that are yet alive" (*The Present State,* 1:38).

35. Translation of *zakashchiki*. The edited draft originally had *proto-popy* (archpriests) (Verkhovskoi, *Uchrezhdenie,* 2, pt. 1: 40).

36. Translation of *blagochinnye.*

37. The text in *Polnoe sobranie zakonov* incorrectly reads: ". . . and not construct necessary buildings. . . ."

38. 1 Corinthians 3:6.

39. 1 Corinthians 3:7 (RSV).

40. 1 Corinthians 4:1–2.

41. None of the early manuscripts or printed editions of the *Spiritual Regulation* has the number "15" here; it first appears in the 1904 edition (Verkhovskoi, *Uchrezhdenie,* 2, pt. 1:43).

42. In the edited draft, the following passage appeared: "But a pastor who is honored in this way, satiated with such glory, comes to regard his whole occupation as consisting of only that he be led about like an untrained horse, but his true vocation he does not know." These words were crossed out, circled, and pasted over with a piece of paper, presumably by Feofan Prokopovich himself. The catchword "untrained," with which a new page began, was scraped away from the bottom of the preceding page. Verkhovskoi first brought this passage to light (ibid., 2, pt. 1:43).

43. 1 Timothy 5:7.

44. The citation is incorrect; the passage is in 2 Corinthians 10:8.

45. 1 Corinthians 5:5.

46. The stipulation about the liturgy did not originally appear in the edited draft (Verkhovskoi, *Uchrezhdenie*, 2, pt. 1:46). According to Tondini, this refers to the third part of the Divine Liturgy, the Liturgy of the Faithful, and is in keeping with the ecclesiastical requirement that the Eucharistic Sacrifice, once begun, must be completed (*Règlement ecclésiastique*, p. 80). For the Liturgy of Saint John Chrysostom and the Liturgy of Saint Basil the Great, see Hapgood, *Service Book*, pp. 67–126.

47. The edited draft originally contained the phrase, ". . . into his house or any other place . . ." (Verkhovskoi, *Uchrezhdenie*, 2, pt. 1: 46).

48. On the practice of excommunicating entire households (*vsedomovnoe otluchenie*), see N. I. Barsov, "Otluchenie" [Excommunication], *Entsiklopedicheskii slovar'*, 43:428–31.

49. Matthew 18:17.

50. 1 Corinthians 5:5.

51. The reference to 1 Corinthians 4:12 is not apt: "And we toil, working with our own hands. We are reviled and we bless, we are persecuted and we bear with it."

52. There obviously exists in this and the next two articles a deviation from the stated topic of episcopal visitations.

53. Disciples of Valentinus, a highly influential second-century leader of the Gnostic movement (P. J. Healy, "Valentinus and Valentinians," *The Catholic Encyclopedia*, 15:256).

54. Followers of the rigidly dualistic religion of the third-century Persian sage Mani (or Manes) (J. P. Arendzen, "Manichaeism," *The Catholic Encyclopedia*, 9:591–97).

55. Cathars, Catharists, or Cathari (from the Greek *katharos*, "pure") is a generic term, which can refer to a number of religious groups or movements (such as the Manicheans) devoted to struggling against what was thought to be impure or corrupt. In the Middle Ages the name was applied to several dualistic sects (N. A. Weber, "Cathari," *The Catholic Encyclopedia*, 3:435–37).

56. Followers of Eutyches, a priest and archimandrite of Constantino-

ple in the second half of the fourth and the first half of the fifth century, whose name became associated with doctrines touching on the nature of Christ (Chapman, "Eutyches," *The Catholic Encyclopedia,* 5:631–33).

57. A group well established in Northern Africa in the fourth century, named after Donatus, bishop of Casae Nigrae. They held that one of the signs of the church is the holiness of its priests and bishops. (Chapman, "Donatists," *The Catholic Encyclopedia,* 5:121–29).

58. Irenaeus, a Greek from Asia Minor who became bishop of Lyons toward the latter part of the second century. He is regarded as one of the Fathers of the Church. His most important work (ca. 180) was the *Refutation and Overthrow of Gnosis, Falsely So Called* (A. Poncelet, "Irenaeus," *The Catholic Encyclopedia,* 8:130–31); "Irenaeus," *The Encyclopedia Britannica,* 12:625); his five books are in Migne, *Patrologiae cursus completus, series graeca,* vol. 7.

59. Epiphanius, bishop of Constantia (Salamis) in the last half of the fourth century, wrote a discourse entitled *Panarion* in which he describes and refutes twenty heresies prior to Christianity and eighty heresies after the appearance of Christianity (P. Canivet, "Epiphanius of Constantia," *New Catholic Encyclopedia,* 5: 478–79).

60. Augustine, bishop of Hippo in the first three decades of the fifth century, wrote against numerous heretics, among them, the Donatists, Manicheans, and Pelagians (E. Portalié, "Augustine," *The Catholic Encyclopedia,* 2:84–104).

61. Theodoret, bishop of Cyrrhus after 423 and until his death ca. 457. He is considered to have been one of the most learned theologians of the fifth century (C. Baur, "Theodoret," *The Catholic Encyclopedia,* 14:574–75; A. von Harnack, "Theodoret," *The Encyclopedia Britannica,* 22:58–59).

62. The name of Arius (died 336), a deacon and priest of Alexandria, became connected with a heresy partly for the solution of which the First Ecumenical Council at Nicaea was convened in 325 (V. C. DeClercq, "Arius" and "Arianism," *New Catholic Encyclopedia,* 1:814 and 791–94).

63. Basil the Great (ca. 330–79), bishop of Caesarea (Migne, *Patrologiae cursus completus, series graeca,* vol. 31, col. 564). On Basil, see J. McSorley, "Basil," *The Catholic Encyclopedia,* 2:330–34.

64. Migne, *Patrologiae cursus completus, series graeca,* vol. 47, col. 319.

65. Gregory of Nazianzus, the Theologian (ca. 329–89), patriarch of Constantinople (ibid., vol. 35, col. 1044). On Gregory, see D. O. Hunter-Blair, "Gregory Nazianzus," *The Catholic Encyclopedia,* 7:10–15.

66. Tondini expresses the opinion that this refers to the king's privilege for the publication of a work, indicated by the phrase "privilège du roi" imprinted in the books of that time (*Règlement ecclésiastique,* p. 121).

67. Tondini concludes that the Latin grammar most closely approximating the one described in the *Spiritual Regulation* was Dom Claude Lancelot's (1615–95) *Nouvelle méthode pour apprendre facilement et en peu de temps la langue latine* (first edition, 1644). A third edition (Paris, 1656) appeared bearing the inscription: *avec privilège de Sa Majesté.* If this selection was too extensive a work to have been the one meant by Prokopovich, Tondini suggests an alternate possibility. The same author, Lancelot, also produced an abridged Latin grammar: *Abrégé de la nouvelle méthode présentée au Roi par MM. de Port-Royal pour apprendre facilement la langue latine* (Paris, 1633) (*Règlement ecclésiastique . . . ,* p. 121).

68. Gregory of Nazianzus (Migne, *Patrologiae cursus completus, series graeca,* vol. 36).

69. Augustine (ibid., *series latina,* vols. 32–47).

70. Athanasius the Great (ca. 296–373), bishop of Alexandria (ibid., *series graeca,* vol. 26). On Athanasius, see C. Clifford, "Athanasius," *The Catholic Encyclopedia,* 2:35–40.

71. Basil (Migne, *Patrologiae cursus completus, series graeca,* vol. 29).

72. Cyril (376–444), bishop of Alexandria (ibid., p. 76). On Cyril, see Chapman, "Cyril," *The Catholic Encyclopedia,* 4:592–95.

73. Leo I, the Great, pope of Rome from 440 to 461 (Migne, *Patrologiae cursus completus, series latina,* vol. 46). On Leo, see J. P. Kirsch, "Leo I," *The Catholic Encyclopedia,* 9:154–57.

74. See note 69 above.

75. Luke 22:32.

76. Verkhovskoi concludes that the reference here is to the second-century Roman historian, Junianus Justinus, who wrote a history adapted from the *Historiae philippicae et totius mundi origines et terras situs* of Pompeius Trogus (*Uchrezhdenie,* 1:442).

77. According to Tondini, here probably is meant Pufendorf's *De officiis hominis et civis juxta legem naturalem,* which Pufendorf himself condensed from his earlier *De jure naturae et gentium* (*Règlement ecclésiastique,* p. 137). The translation of this article follows the text of the edited draft, as given by Verkhovskoi in *Uchrezhdenie,* in which the use of Pufendorf's work is unequivocally prescribed. This same passage in *Polnoe sobranie zakonov* can be interpreted, primarily because of a difference in punctuation, as attaching a condition on such use: "Pufendorf's abridged politics, if it is considered applicable, and it can be added to dialectics."

78. The following words were crossed out in the edited draft: ". . . as we can see from our own experience and from that of others" (Verkhovskoi, *Uchrezhdenie,* 1:445).

79. Verkhovskoi is led to conclude that, while the graduates of schools in bishops' houses (articles 9–13, "Matters Pertaining to Bishops") were intended primarily to become priests or monks, those who

graduated from the Academy or the Seminary were to have state service as their principal goal (ibid., 1:402).

80. 1 Corinthians 1:12–13.

81. 1 Corinthians 4:6.

82. The text in *Polnoe sobranie zakonov* is incorrect: "our" should read *your,* as it does in the translation. The passage was correct in the edited draft.

83. 1 Corinthians 3:6.

84. John 3:16.

85. 1 John 2:15–16.

86. Cf. 1 John 2:12–13.

87. 1 Corinthians 2:14–15: "But the sensual man does not perceive the things that are of the Spirit of God, for it is foolishness to him and he cannot understand, because it is examined spiritually. But the spiritual man judges all things, and he himself is judged by no man."

88. 1 Peter 2:9.

89. Apocalypse 5:10.

90. 1 Corinthians 11:26.

91. John 6:54.

92. 1 Corinthians 10:16–17.

93. In the edited draft, this article concluded as follows: ". . . likewise, it may seek judgment against them in the Senate." This concluding statement was rescinded when the *Spiritual Regulation* underwent examination in February 1720; subsequently, additional provisions having to do with the procedures to be observed in conducting a spiritual investigation were added to it.

94. Feofan Prokopovich personally added here the following instruction in the margin of the fourth draft (*Tipografskaia rukopis'* [The Printing Plant Manuscript]) of the *Spiritual Regulation:* "In Article 6 of the 'Rules for Laymen' in the *Spiritual Regulation,* print this as a note in small letters—'A printed ukase of Our Great Sovereign concerning this was promulgated in 1718.'" The reference, according to Verkhovskoi, is to the ukases of 17 February and 16 March 1718; see *Polnoe sobranie zakonov,* 5:544–45, no. 3169; pp. 554–55, no. 3183 (*Uchrezhdenie,* 1:464).

95. Household churches, or chapels, were absolutely forbidden by Peter's personal ukase of 19 February 1718 (*Polnoe sobranie zakonov,* 5:545–46). Even in Peter's time, however, corporals (silk cloths spread out upon an altar during the celebration of mass), as well as other items necessary for divine services, were once again allowed to be kept in the houses of notable or elderly persons in extreme cases, though they were not to have their own personal clergy. The prohibition against household churches was annulled in 1762 ("Tserkvi domovyia" [Household Churches], *Entsiklopedicheskii slovar',* 75:62).

96. Galatians 3:28.

97. Genesis 3:19.

98. The citation to Ephesians 5 is incorrect. The reference should be to Ephesians 4:28: "He who was wont to steal, let him steal no longer, but rather let him labor, working with his hands at what is good, that he may have something to share with him who suffers need."

99. 2 Thessalonians 3:10.

100. Immediately below the text of the *Spiritual Regulation* come the names of the signatories to it. For the purpose of signing the document, two final drafts were prepared from Prokopovich's rough draft. Peter had ordered these two drafts specially made so that one of them could remain safely in the capital while the other was taken throughout the country for prominent churchmen to sign (S. G. Runkevich, *Istoriia Russkoi Tserkvi pod upravlenium sviatieishago Sinoda* [The History of the Russian Church under the Administration of the Most Holy Synod], p. 121; Verkhovskoi, *Uchrezhdenie, 2, pt. 1:20*).

Final Draft I: The following signatures were inscribed on the copy retained for safekeeping (as listed by Verkhovskoi, *Uchrezhdenie, 2*, pt. 1:19). In this draft the names appear in two columns: on the left side of the page are the names of the eight initial ecclesiastical signatories; on the right, those of seven senators (forming a majority of one from the total Senate membership of thirteen), followed by Peter's. Asterisks (not in the original) designate members of the subsequently established Spiritual College.

(1) The left column: * Humble Stefan, Unworthy Metropolitan of Riazan'; Humble Sil'vestr, Metropolitan of Smolensk; * Humble Feofan, Bishop of Pskov; Humble Pitirim, Bishop of Nizhnii-Novgorod; Humble Varlaam, Bishop of Tver'; Humble Aaron, Bishop of Karelia; * Feodosii, Archimandrite of the Alexander Nevsky [Monastery in Saint Petersburg]; Antonii, Archimandrite of the [Moscow] Zlatoustov [Monastery].

(2) The right column: Admiral Graf Apraksin; Kanzler Graf Golovkin; Prince Iakov Dolgorukoi; Prince Dmitrii Golitsyn; Graf Andrei Matvieev; Peter Tal'stoi [i.e., Tolstoy]; Baron Peter Shafirov; PETER.

On verso of the signature sheet, there follow five additional names of clergymen who apparently signed this first draft at a later time (crosses, not in the original, denote those who signed *only* this first draft and not the second, as did all others, laymen and clergy, whose names appear here): Iona Sal'nikieev, Archimandrite of the Kazan' Transfiguration of the Savior Monastery; * Peter, Archimandrite of the Moscow Simonov Monastery; + Humble Pakhomii, Metropolitan of Voronezh and Elets; + * Gavriil [Buzhinsky], Archimandrite of the [Moscow] Ipatsky Monastery; + * Ierofei [Prilutsky], Archimandrite of the [Moscow] Donskoi Monastery.

There are no other signatories to the *Spiritual Regulation* in the first final draft.

Final Draft II: The same eight ranking hierarchs and seven senators who signed at the beginning of the list of signatures in the first draft also signed the second. Only the sequence in which their names appear differs slightly from that in the first draft. The most notable difference is the location of Peter's name, which in this second draft precedes all the rest, being placed above that of Stefan Iavorsky at the very top of the left-hand column.

After this second draft had been signed in Saint Petersburg on 27 February 1720, it was taken in the following months to Moscow and elsewhere for the collection of other clerical signatures. When it was returned to the Senate at the start of the next year, it bore the signatures of a total of eighty-four clergymen (plus, of course, those of the seven senators). Since there were three clergymen who had signed only the first draft, the grand total of individual ecclesiastical signatories to the *Spiritual Regulation* is eighty-seven.

101. For a description of the four manuscripts of the Supplement to the *Spiritual Regulation*, see Verkhovskoi, *Uchrezhdenie*, 2, pt. 1: 77–81.

102. The initial version of the Supplement in all cases made reference to the Spiritual College instead of to the Most Holy Ruling Synod (ibid., 2, pt. 1:83 ff.).

103. The reference is to Paul's discourse at Miletus, Acts 20:17–38.

104. In 1 Timothy 3:1–13, St. Paul describes the qualities to be sought for in bishops and deacons.

105. Titus 1:5–16 refers to St. Paul's pastoral charge to Titus in connection with the latter's mission in Crete.

106. Peter here added a note in the edited draft in which he required that there be incorporated provisions for: (1) an oath of loyalty to the Sovereign, in addition to the oath already specified in this article; and (2) the reporting by priests of intentions inimical to the Sovereign that may be revealed in confession. As a result, articles 11 and 12 as contained in the translation were added, while articles 11 and 12 of the original manuscript were renumbered (Verkhovskoi, *Uchrezhdenie*, 1:477; 2, pt. 1:84–92; Runkevich, *Istoriia Russkoi Tserkvi*, p. 158.

107. *Polnoe sobranie zakonov*, 6, no. 3984:666.

108. Matthew 18:15.

109. Matthew 18:17 (RSV).

110. Although Matthew 18:16 is cited in the footnote as the source for a quotation, this verse is not actually quoted in the *Spiritual Regulation*.

111. The Most Holy Synod's announcement of 17 May 1722 to the spiritual and priestly rank, referred to in the following sentence of the Supplement, mentions three specific cases in this regard: 1) that of the scribe Grigorii Talitsky, who in 1700 confessed under torture to defaming the tsar and harboring the intention of inciting popular disobedience and insurrection through the dissemination of printed materials; 2) that of Peter's son, Tsarevich Alexis, around whom in 1718 Peter had

grown to suspect the concentration of an extensive plot against him and his reforms; and 3) that of the rather muddled Old-Believer monk from Penza, Varlaam (formerly captain of dragoons Vasilii Levin), who was accused in March 1722 of publicly maligning the tsar—this latter case is the one referred to in the present article of the Supplement as having occurred "this year." Talitsky and Varlaam were executed; Alexis died under mysterious circumstances. In all these cases members of the clergy were implicated; and in the latter two, it was asserted by the authorities that the confessors of the accused had obtained advance knowledge in the confessional of the purported conspiratorial plots. For the history of these incidents, see Soloviev, *Istoriia Rossii,* 8:100–102; 9:105–91, 513.

112. On 17 May 1722, four days after Peter had left Saint Petersburg on his Persian campaign, the Most Holy Ruling Synod issued an announcement to the spiritual and priestly rank (*Polnoe sobranie zakonov,* 6:685–89, no. 4012). It put forward three sets of stipulations. But before addressing itself to them, it presented as background information the three cases of imputed treasonous activity described in the preceding note. It then moved on to the matters at hand.

First, it authorized, justified, and encouraged disclosure by the clergy of intended crimes revealed to them when confession was not accompanied by repentance and renunciation of the intended deed. This part of the announcement corresponds word for word to nearly all of Article 11 in the Supplement, from "If someone in confession informs his spiritual father . . ." to ". . . is an insidious contrivance for the seduction of his own conscience." By issuing this announcement the Synod, under Peter's orders, sought to obviate any further delay in implementing the procedure for submitting confessional reports until the *Spiritual Regulation* and its Supplement would be ready (the second time) for distribution.

A special oath for the clergy was the second matter dealt with by this announcement. The first part of the oath is similar to that for the members of the Spiritual College (see pp. 5–6 of this translation); the second part, beginning with "To this also do I obligate myself . . .," is directed to the fulfillment of their duties by priests in accordance with their charters of ordination, the provisions of the *Spiritual Regulation,* and the terms of the present Synodal announcement in regard to submitting confessional reports. The oath also fixed restrictions on the priests' relations with schismatics.

The third concern of the synodal announcement of 17 May was with the responsibility of confessors to report false miracles. Here it corresponds word for word with Article 12 of the Supplement (see pp. 62–63 of the present translation).

113. Exodus 20:7; Deuteronomy 5:11.

114. *Trebnik* [The Book of Needs], containing, among others, the rites for the administration of penance and Holy Communion.

115. The first paragraph of this article closely followed the wording

of a note added by Peter to Article 11 of the edited draft (Article 13 of the present translation). The subsequent provisions of this article were an elaboration of the content of that note (Verkhovskoi, *Uchrezhdenie*, 2, pt. 1:85).

116. Migne, *Patrologiae cursus completus series graeca*, vol. 45, col. 221. On Gregory (ca. 331–96), see R. F Harvanek, "Gregory of Nyssa, Saint," *New Catholic Encyclopedia*, 6:794–96.

117. Dübner, *Sancti Joannis Chrysostomi Opera Selecta*, vol. 1.

118. Jeremiah 3:3 (RSV).

119. The Trullan Council, or Council *in Trullo* (from the Greek *troullos*, "dome," "cupola"), was convoked in 691 in Constantinople to bring about a settlement of issues remaining in the wake of the Fifth and Sixth Ecumenical Councils (Vasiliev, *History of the Byzantine Empire*, 1:225).

120. Theodore Balsamon, patriarch of Antioch in the second half of the twelfth century, who became a noted Greek canonist, following in the footsteps of the earlier John Zonaras (ibid., 2:470).

121. John Zonaras, a twelfth-century Byzantine theologian, historian, and commentator on canon law (R. Browning, "Zonaras, John," *New Catholic Encyclopedia*, 14:1129).

122. Alexis Aristenos, a twelfth-century Byzantine canonist ("Aristin," *Novyi entsiklopedicheskii slovar'* [The New Encyclopedic Dictionary], 3:487; F. Chalandon, *Jean II Comnène et Manuel I Comnène*, 2:19, 28).

123. Hebrews 10:23.

124. The edited draft contained the following clause: ". . . children born out of wedlock are baptized for the sake of concealing it." This passage was withdrawn in conformity with Peter's notation: "It does not seem necessary" (Runkevich, *Istoriia Russkoi Tserkvi*, p. 159).

125. The sanctions in this article were prescribed by Peter personally in the edited draft (Verkhovskoi, *Uchrezhdenie*, 1:483).

126. Verkhovskoi sees a connection between this article and the beginning in Russia after 1716 of a corps of military chaplains, having its own administration separate from the traditional eparchial organization, whose administrative control became undermined when priests were enabled to enter military service without the consent of their bishops (ibid., 1:485).

127. Matthew 19:5.

128. Eustathius, bishop of Sebaste (died ca. 380), in about the middle of the fourth century founded a strict monastic sect whose followers were condemned by the Council of Gangra, ca. 340 ("Evstafii Sevatiisky" [Eustathius of Sebaste], *Entsiklopedicheskii slovar'*, 11:505; "Gangrsky sobor" [The Council of Gangra], *Novyi entsiklopedicheskii slovar'*, 12:591; A. Fortescue, "Eustathius of Sebaste," *The Catholic Encyclopedia*, 5:628–29).

129. Translation of *prikaznye chelovieki*.

130. Translation of *gubernator*.

131. An older title from the Muscovite period for a provincial administrator, or governor.

132. Translation of *prikashchiki*.

133. On tonsure in Russia, see Verkhovskoi, *Uchrezhdenie*, 1:509; and "Postrizhenie" [Tonsure], *Entsiklopedicheskii slovar'*, 48:712; and for a related study see N. N. Pal'mov, *Postrizhenie v monashestvo; chiny postrizheniia v monashestvo v grecheskoi tserkvi* [Tonsuring into the Monastic Life; the Rites of Tonsuring into the Monastic Life in the Greek Church].

134. Intoned by the priest in the liturgy at the elevation (Hapgood, *Service Book*, p. 114).

135. Said by the priest or deacon to summon those in the congregation who are to receive Communion (ibid., p. 119).

136. *Kvas* (kvass, quass), a mildly alcoholic beverage, resembling sour beer, of which Consett gives a picturesque description: "Quass, the most general Liquor of the Country, which is a kind of small Beer made of Wheat-Bran, the Flower of Rye, and of Rye-Malt, which being mash'd together, with hot Water, into a Consistence, like a Pudding, are set into an Oven for a Night in a Pot. Next day this mixture, taken out of the Pot almost crusted, is put into a Tub, and warm Water added to it, with sower Leaven at the same time, which causes it to ferment, and when it has work'd up to the top they begin to drink it; and as it begins to drink too sower, more warm Water is pour'd on, 'till the Strength of the Ingredients is spent. It is quenching, and may pass for an agreeable Liquor, to such as do not dislike a very small Beer. The Russes have now learn'd to malt Barley, and tho the Grain is but small, yet makes a very good Malt, and good Table Beer, which is publickly sold in their Tipling Houses, or Cabacks" (*The Present State*, 1:169).

137. The final phrase is Peter's (Runkevich, *Istoriia Russkoi Tserkvi*, p. 161).

138. This article, not present in the edited draft, was added at Peter's personal direction (Verkhovskoi, *Uchrezhdenie*, 2, pt. 1:99–100; Runkevich, *Istoriia Russkoi Tserkvi*, p. 161).

139. The remainder of this article is almost a literal rendering of Peter's note in the margin of the edited draft, except for the final sentence, added by the Synod (Verkhovskoi, *Uchrezhdenie*, 2, pt. 1:100; Runkevich, *Istoriia Russkoi Tserkvi*, p. 161).

140. In the edited draft, between the words "people" and "where," this article read: ". . . the bishop shall assign them a special place. . . ." Peter's note in the margin designated specific locations where the nuns were to remain during services (ibid.).

141. 1 Timothy 5:9.

142. A contemporary of Saint Anthony (see the following note), Paul the Hermit fled at the age of sixteen into the desert of the Thebaid dur-

ing the Decian persecution (F. J. Bacchus, "Paul the Hermit, Saint," *The Catholic Encyclopedia*, 11:590–91).

143. Saint Anthony (ca. 251–356) is generally regarded as the founder of Christian monasticism (E. C. Butler, "Anthony, Saint," *The Catholic Encyclopedia*, 1:553–55).

144. Macarius of Egypt, known also as Macarius the Great (301–91), a Father of the Church, fled to the Egyptian desert at the age of thirty and was there later made presbyter to the people who followed him (Barsov, "Makarii Velikii" [Macarius the Great], *Entsiklopedicheskii slovar'*, 35:395–96). Some of his writings, of a homiletic character, have survived; see Migne, *Patrologiae cursus completus, series graeca*, vol. 34.

145. Except for the phrase, ". . . and other warm countries," added by the Synod, the remainder of this article follows exactly Peter's note in the margin of the edited draft (Runkevich, *Istoriia Russkoi Tserkvi*, pp. 161–62).

146. The addition of this parenthetical elaboration was ordered by Peter (ibid., p. 162).

147. In *Polnoe sobranie zakonov* the top line of the first column on page 714 is erroneously transposed from its correct position at the top of the first column on page 715.

148. *Polnoe sobranie zakonov*, vol. 6, no. 3485, dated 13 January 1720.

149. At this point the same original members of Synod, who had earlier signed the Oath of the Members of the Spiritual College (see p. 103, n.5, and pp. 5–6 of the translation), also signed the (first) final draft of the Supplement. Unlike the oath, however, the date of this signing is uncertain. Internal evidence suggests that it was signed some time after 31 December 1720 (when Prokopovich was elevated to archbishop) and in or before March 1721 (when Osvianikov, who still signs here as hieromonk, was promoted to hegumen). Peter Grigor'ev appears here as protopope of the Cathedral of Saints Peter and Paul.

These same eleven signatures also appeared in the first printed edition of the Supplement, published together with the 16 September 1721 edition of the *Spiritual Regulation*.

It should be noted that the point at which these signatures appeared in the Supplement's first edition corresponded to the end of Article 61 (not 62, as in the present translation). This happened because, after the first edition of the Supplement had been published, the numeration of articles was altered (Article 61 thus becoming 62) by Peter's corrections to the first edition, including the addition of Article 11 (as it appears in the present translation on pp. 60–62)

All the signatures are listed in Verkhovskoi, *Uchrezhdenie*, 1:206; 2, pt. 1:104, n. 156.

150. Translation of *Kormchaia kniga*, a collection primarily but not

exclusively of canon law, derived from various sources, but initially from the Greek *Nomokanon,* which was brought from Byzantium into Kievan Rus' by missionaries upon the introduction of Christianity at the end of the tenth century. The *Book of the Rudder* served as a guide for both ecclesiastical and civil judges; for that reason it included both kinds of laws taken from Byzantine originals. In time, articles of Russian provenience came to be included also. For the later inclusions into this legislation and its influence upon the development of Russian law, see V. O. Kliuchevsky, *Sochineniia v vos'mi tomakh* [Works in eight volumes], 1:209–10; M. N. Tikhomirov, *Istochnikovedenie istorii SSSR* [A Study of Sources for the History of the USSR], 1:85.

151. At this point are found signatures to the (second) final draft manuscript of the Supplement, approved by the following members of the Synod, eight clergymen and one layman (technically only a staff member), on some unspecified day late in April or early in May 1722 (the names are from Verkhovskoi, *Uchrezhdenie,* 2, pt. 1:104–5, n. 156). The names of layman Timofei Palekhin and Archimandrite Feofilakt Lopatinsky make their first appearance in a synodal list, the former as a recently appointed ober-secretary, the latter as councilor. The names of Buzhinsky, Prilutsky, Smielich, and Osvianikov are associated with higher ranks or posts than they held before. Missing from this list are the names of four clergymen who had signed the (first) final draft of the Supplement in early 1721; but their signatures are entered in the *printed* copies of this edition of the Supplement (see the following note). Hence, the entire original membership of the Synod signed this edition of the Supplement, either in its manuscript or printed form. The signatures on the manuscript are:

Stefan [Iavorsky], Metropolitan of Riazan'; Feodosii [Ianovsky], Archbishop of Novgorod and Archimandrite of the Alexander Nevsky [Monastery in Saint Petersburg]; Feofan [Prokopovich], Archbishop of Pskov; Gavriil [Buzhinsky], Archimandrite of the Trinity-Sergius Monastery; Feofilakt [Lopatinsky], Archimandrite of the Miracles [Monastery in Moscow]; Ierofei [Prilutsky], Archimandrite of the [Moscow] New Savior [Monastery]; Peter [Smielich], Archimandrite of the [Moscow] Simonov [Monastery]; Varlaam [Osvianikov], Hegumen of [the Saint Nicholas Monastery on the] Ugriesha [River]; Ober-Secretary Timofei Palekhin.

152 The 14 June 1722 printed edition of the Supplement (issued for distribution with the second edition of the *Spiritual Regulation* on 28 September 1722) contains the signatures of six members of the Synod; it also contains the nine signatures listed in the preceding note—those that had been affixed to the manuscript draft of this same edition (taken from Verkhovskoi, *Uchrezhdenie,* 2, pt. 1:105, n. 156). The names of two new assessors, Feofan Krulik and Anastasii Nausii, make their first appearance in a synodal list; those of Leonid and Afanasii (formerly Ana-

stasios Kontoeidēs) are associated with higher ranks or posts than in previous lists.

The six members of the Synod who signed were: Leonid, Archbishop of Krutitsy; Afanasii, Hegumen of the Tolgsky [Monastery near Iaroslavl']; Hieromonk Feofan Krulik; Ioann [Simeonov], Protopresbyter of the Trinity [Cathedral in Saint Petersburg]; Peter [Grigor'ev], Protopresbyter of the [Cathedral of Saints] Peter and Paul [in Saint Petersburg]; Anastasii Nausii.

Thus a total of fourteen clergymen and one layman signed the final version of the Supplement.

𝕭ibliography

PUBLISHED COLLECTIONS
OF DOCUMENTS AND OTHER SOURCE MATERIALS

Akty, sobrannye v bibliotekakh i arkhivakh Rossiiskoi imperii Arkheo-graficheskoiu ekspeditsieiu Imperatorskoi Akademii nauk [Records Collected in the Libraries and Archives of the Russian Empire by the Archaeographical Expedition of the Imperial Academy of Sciences]. 4 vols. St. Petersburg, 1836.

Beneshevich, V. N., ed. *Sbornik pamiatnikov po istorii tserkovnago prava, preimushchestvenno Russkoi Tserkvi do epokhi Petra Velikago* [A Collection of Monuments on the History of Ecclesiastical Law, Principally of the Russian Church to the Period of Peter the Great]. 2 vols. Petrograd, 1914–15.

Consett, Thomas, ed. *The Present State and Regulations of the Church of Russia.* 2 vols. London: J. Brotherton, 1729.

Dübner, Friedrich, ed. *Sancti Joannis Chrysostomi Opera Selecta.* Paris: A. Firmin Didot, 1861.

Ger'e (Guerrier), V. I., ed. *Sbornik pisem i memorialov Leibnitsa otno-siashchikhsia k Rossii i Petru Velikomu* [A Collection of Leibnitz' Letters and Memorials Concerning Russia and Peter the Great]. St. Petersburg, 1873.

Hapgood, Isabel F., ed. *Service Book of the Holy Orthodox-Catholic Apostolic Church.* 3rd ed. Brooklyn : Syrian Antiochian Orthodox Archdiocese, 1956.

The Holy Bible: New Catholic Edition. New York: Catholic Book Publishing Co., 1957.

[123]

The Holy Bible: Revised Standard Version. New York: Harper, 1952.

Iavorsky, Stefan. "Poslanie Stefana Iavorskago, mitropolita riazanskago i muromskago, . . . ob uchenii ieromonakha Feofana Prokopovicha" [The Epistle of Stefan Iavorsky, metropolitan of Riazan' and Murom, . . . on the Teaching of Hieromonk Feofan Prokopovich]. Contributed by Archimandrite Makarii. *Chteniia v Imperatorskom Obshchestvie istorii i drevnostei rossiiskikh* [Readings Before the Imperial Society of Russian History and Antiquities] 4 (1864): 5–8.

———. "Slovo pred prokliatiem Mazepy, proiznesennoe mitropolitom Stefanom Iavorskim v Moskovskom Uspenskom soborie, 12 noiabria 1708 g." [The Sermon at the Anathematization of Mazepa, Delivered by Metropolitan Stefan Iavorsky in the Cathedral of the Assumption in Moscow on 12 November 1708]. *Trudy Kievskoi dukhovnoi akademii* [Transactions of the Kiev Theological Academy], December 1865, pp. 499–512.

Lebedev, V. I., ed. *Reformy Petra I. Sbornik dokumentov* [The Reforms of Peter I. A Collection of Documents]. Moscow, 1937.

Leonid, archimandrite, ed. "Perepiska Tsaria Petra s Patriarkhom Adrianom" [Tsar Peter's Correspondence With Patriarch Adrian]. *Chteniia v Imperatorskom Obshchestvie istorii i drevnostei rossiiskikh,* 4 (1876): 238–43.

Malvy, Antoine, and Marcel Viller, eds. "La Confession Orthodoxe de Pierre Moghila." *Orientalia Christiana,* vol. 10, no. 39. Rome: Pont. Institutum Orientalium Studiorum, 1927.

Migne, Jacques-Paul, ed. *Patrologiae cursus completus, seu bibliotheca universalis, integra, uniformis, commoda, oeconomica, omnium SS. patrum, doctorum scriptorumque ecclesiasticorum sive latinorum, sive graecorum . . . series graeca.* 162 vols. Paris: J.-P. Migne, 1857–86.

———. *Patrologiae cursus completus, . . . series latina.* 221 vols. Paris: J.-P. Migne, 1841–93.

Percival, Henry R., ed. *The Seven Ecumenical Councils of the Undivided Church. Their Canons and Dogmatic Decrees, Together With the Canons of All the Local Synods Which Have Received Ecumenical Acceptance.* New York: Charles Scribner's Sons, 1900.

Pis'ma i bumagi Imperatora Petra Velikogo [Letters and Papers of Emperor Peter the Great]. 11 vols. in 17. St. Petersburg, Moscow-Leningrad, Moscow: 1887–1964.

Polnoe sobranie zakonov Rossiiskoi imperii s 1649 goda [The Complete Collection of the Laws of the Russian Empire From 1649]. 1st series. 46 vols. in 48 and 3 appendixes. St. Petersburg, 1830–43.

Prokopovich, Feofan. "From 'The Spiritual Reglement.'" In *Anthology of Russian Literature* 1:212–14. Edited by Leo Wiener. 1902. Reprint. New York: Benjamin Blom, 1967.

————. "Materialy dlia istorii russkoi religioznoi i tserkovnoi zhizni. (Pis'ma Feofana Prokopovicha.) Pis'mo k Iakovu Markovichu iz Peterburga ot 10 maia 1720 g." [Materials for the History of Russian Religious and Ecclesiastical Life. (The Letters of Feofan Prokopovich.) Letter to Iakov Markovich From Petersburg, Dated 10 May 1720]. *Trudy Kievskoi dukhovnoi akademii,* February 1865, pp. 287–94.

————. *Sochineniia* [Works], ed. I. P. Eremin. Moscow and Leningrad, 1961.

————. "Vyderzhki iz rukopisnoi retoriki F. Prokopovicha, soderzhashchiia v sebie izobrazhenie papistov i iezuitov" [Excerpts From the Written Rhetoric of F. Prokopovich, Containing a Depiction of Papists and Jesuits]. *Trudy Kievskoi dukhovnoi akademii,* April 1865, pp. 614–37.

Stoglav. Sobor byvshii v Moskvie pri Velikom gosudarie tsarie i Velikom kniazie Ivanie Vasil'evichie (v lieto 7059) [The Hundred Chapters. The Council Held in Moscow Under Our Great Sovereign, Tsar and Grand Prince, Ivan Vasil'evich (in the Year 7059)]. London: Trübner & Co., 1860.

Tondini, Césaire, ed. *Dukhovnyi reglament po moskovskomu izdaniiu 1861 g. (v Sinodal'noi tipografii) rachitel'no sravnennomu s izdaniem Polnago sobraniia zakonov* [The Spiritual Regulation According to the Moscow Edition of 1861 (in the Synodal Printing-house), Carefully Compared With the Version in the Complete Collection of Laws]. Brussels and London: Burns & Oates, 1874.

————. *Règlement ecclésiastique de Pierre le Grand, traduit en français sur le russe avec introduction et notes.* Paris: Librairie de la Société Bibliographique, 1874.

Verkhovskoi, P. V., ed. "Manifest 25-go ianvaria 1721 g."; "Prisiaga chlenov Dukhovnoi kollegii"; "Dukhovnyi reglament"; "Pribavlenie k Dukhovnomu reglamentu" [The Manifesto of 25 January 1721; the Oath of the Members of the Spiritual College; the Spiritual Regulation; the Supplement to the Spiritual Regulation]. In *Uchrezhdenie Dukhovnoi kollegii i Dukhovnyi reglament. K voprosu ob otnoshenii Tserkvi i gosudarstva v Rossii* [The Establishment of the Spiritual College and the Spiritual Regulation. On the Question of the Relations of Church and State in Russia] 2, pt. 1:3–105. Rostov-on-the-Don, 1916.

Voskresensky, N. A., ed. *Zakonodatel'nye akty Petra I* [Legislative Enactments of Peter I], vol. 1. Moscow and Leningrad, 1945.

HISTORIES, BIOGRAPHIES, JOURNALS, AND REFERENCE WORKS

"Adrian." *Chteniia v Imperatorskom Obshchestvie istorii i drevnostei rossiiskikh* 8 (1848): 29–36.

Amburger, Erik. *Geschichte der Behördenorganisation Russlands von Peter der Grossen bis 1917.* Leiden: E. J. Brill, 1966.

Andreev, A. I., ed. *Petr Velikii. Sbornik statei* [Peter the Great. A Collection of Articles]. Moscow and Leningrad, 1947.

Ardashev, P. "Absoliutizm" [Absolutism]. *Novyi entsiklopedicheskii slovar'* [The New Encyclopedic Dictionary] 1: cols. 81–89. 29 vols. St. Petersburg: Brokgauz & Efron, 1911.

Arendzen, J. P. "Manichaeism." *The Catholic Encyclopedia* 9:591–97.

Bacchus, F. J. "Paul the Hermit, Saint." *The Catholic Encyclopedia* 11: 590–91.

Barsov, N. I. "Lichnost' Feofana Prokopovicha" [The Personality of Feofan Prokopovich]. *Istoricheskie, kriticheskie i polemicheskie opyty* [Historical, Critical, and Polemical Studies], pp. 114–27. St. Petersburg, 1879.

———. "Otluchenie" [Excommunication]. *Entsiklopedicheskii slovar'* 43: 429–31.

Barsov, T. V. *Konstantinpol'skii patriarkh i ego vlast' nad Russkoiu Tserkoviiu* [The Patriarch of Constantinople and His Authority Over the Russian Church]. 1878. Reprint. The Hague and Paris: Mouton, 1968.

———. *Sinodal'nyia uchrezhdeniia prezhniago vremeni* [Synodal Institutions of Former Times]. St. Petersburg, 1897.

———. *Sviatieishii sinod v ego proshlom* [The Most Holy Synod in Its Past]. St. Petersburg, 1896.

Baur, C. "John Chrysostom." *The Catholic Encyclopedia* 8:452–57.

———. "Theodoret." *The Catholic Encyclopedia* 14: 574–75.

Bieliaev, I. S. "Ikotniki i klikushki" [Hiccoughers and Squawlers]. *Russkaia starina,* April 1905, pp. 144–63.

Bielogostitsky, V. V. "Reforma Petra Velikago po vysshemu tserkovnomu upravleniiu" [Peter the Great's Reform of the Church's Higher Administration]. *Zhurnal Ministerstva narodnago prosvieshcheniia,* June 1892, pp. 257–81; July 1892, pp. 1–23.

Bissonnette, Georges L. "Pufendorf and the Church Reforms of Peter the Great." Ph.D. dissertation, Columbia University, 1962.

Bogoslovsky, M. M. "Dietstvo Petra Velikago" [Peter the Great's Childhood]. *Russkaia starina,* January 1917, pp. 5–29.

———. *Petr I. Materialy dlia biografii* [Peter I. Materials for a Biography]. 5 vols. Moscow, 1940–48.

————. "Petr Velikii" [Peter the Great]. In *Tri vieka* 3:15–33.

————. *Petr Velikii i ego reforma* [Peter the Great and His Reform]. Moscow, 1920.

Brikner, Aleksandr. "Fr.-Khr. Veber" [Fr. Chr. Weber]. *Zhurnal Ministerstva narodnago prosvieshcheniia.* January 1881, pp. 45–78; February 1881, pp. 179–221.

Browning, R. "Zonaras, John." *New Catholic Encyclopedia* 14:1129.

Butler, E. C. "Anthony, Saint." *The Catholic Encyclopedia* 1:553–55.

Canivet, P. "Epiphanius of Constantia." *New Catholic Encyclopedia* 5: 478–79.

The Catholic Encyclopedia, ed. C. G Herberman et al. 18 vols. New York: The Encyclopedia Press, 1913.

Chalandon, Ferdinand. *Jean II Comnène et Manuel I Comnène.* 2 vols. Reprint. New York: B. Franklin, 1960.

Chapman, J. "Cyril." *The Catholic Encyclopedia* 4: 592–95.

————. "Donatists." *The Catholic Encyclopedia* 5 121–29.

————. "Eutyches." *The Catholic Encyclopedia* 5: 531–33.

————. "Monarchians." *The Catholic Encyclopedia* 10: 448–51.

————. "Nestorius." *The Catholic Encyclopedia* 10: 755–59.

Chistovich, I. A. *Feofan Prokopovich i ego vremia* [Feofan Prokopovich and His Time]. St. Petersburg, 1868.

Chuchmarev, V. G. V. *Leibnits i russkaia kul'tura* [G. W. Leibnitz and Russian Culture]. Moscow, 1968.

Clifford, C. "Athanasius." *The Catholic Encyclopedia* 2: 35–40.

Cracraft, James. *The Church Reform of Peter the Great.* Stanford: Stanford University Press, 1971.

Cross, Frank L., ed. *The Oxford Dictionary of the Christian Church.* London and New York: Oxford University Press, 1957.

DeClercq, V. C. "Arius" and "Arianism." *New Catholic Encyclopedia* 1: 814, 791–94.

D'iakonov, M. A. *Vlast' moskovskikh gosudarei. Ocherki iz istorii politicheskikh idei drevnei Rusi do kontsa XVI vieka* [The Authority of the Muscovite Sovereigns. Essays on the Political Ideas of Early Rus' to the End of the Sixteenth Century]. St. Petersburg, 1889.

Dunn, A. [H. Weedon]. *A Pilgrim's Guide to Rome.* New York: Prentice-Hall, 1950.

Entsiklopedicheskii slovar' [The Encyclopedic Dictionary]. 82 vols. St. Petersburg: Brokgauz & Efron, 1896.

Filaret, archbishop of Chernigov. *Istoriia Russkoi Tserkvi* [History of the Russian Church]. 5th ed. 5 vols. Moscow, 1888.

Florovsky, Georges. *Puti russkago bogosloviia* [The Paths of Russian Theology]. Paris, 1937.

————. Review of "Ocherki po istorii Russkoi Tserkvi" [Essays on the History of the Russian Church] by A. V. Kartashev. *Slavic Review* 23 (1964): 574–78.

Fortescue, A. "Eustathius of Sebaste." *The Catholic Encyclopedia* 5: 628–29.

Ger'e (Guerrier), V. I. "Otnosheniia Leibnitsa k Petru Velikomu" [Leibnitz' Relations With Peter the Great]. *Zhurnal Ministerstva narodnago prosvieshcheniia,* January 1870, pp. 1–48; February 1870, pp. 345–415; April 1870, pp. 309–90.

Golikov, I. I. *Dieianiia Petra Velikago* [The Deeds of Peter the Great]. 2d ed. 15 vols. Moscow, 1837–43.

Golubinsky, E. E. *Istoriia Russkoi Tserkvi* [History of the Russian Church]. 2 vols. in 4. Moscow, 1880–1917.

————. "O reformie v bytie Russkoi Tserkvi" [On Reform in Russian Church Life]. *Chteniia v Imperatorskom Obshchestvie istorii i drevnostei rossiiskikh,* 3 (1913): i–xii, 1–132.

Gorchakov, M. I. "Monastyrskii prikaz" [The Central Administrative Agency of Monasteries]. *Entsiklopedicheskii slovar'* 38:708–12.

————. *O zemel'nykh vladieniiakh rossiiskikh mitropolitov, patriarkhov i Sviatieishago sinoda, 988–1738* [On the Land Holdings of Russian Metropolitans, Patriarchs, and the Most Holy Synod, 988–1738]. St. Petersburg, 1871.

————. "Sinod" [The Synod]. *Entsiklopedicheskii slovar'* 59: 38–43.

"Gosudarstvennyia idei Petra Velikago i ikh sud'ba. 30-go maia 1672 —30-go maia 1872 g." [Peter the Great's Ideas Concerning the State and Their Fate. 30 May 1672–30 May 1872]. *Viestnik Evropy* [Messenger of Europe] 6 (June 1872): 770–96.

Grégoire, Henri. "The Byzantine Church." In *Byzantium: An Introduction to East Roman Civilization,* ed. N. H. Baynes and H. St. L. B. Moss, pp. 86–135. Oxford: Oxford University Press, 1961.

Grey, Ian. *Peter the Great, Emperor of All Russia.* Philadelphia and New York: J. B. Lippincott Co., 1960.

Guber, Petr. "Absoliutizm i pravoslavie" [Absolutism and Orthodoxy]. *Russkaia mysl'* [Russian Thought] 2 (1913): 111–24.

Gurvich, G. D. *"Pravda voli monarshei" F. Prokopovicha i eia zapadnoevropeiskie istochniki* [F. Prokopovich's "Justice of the Monarch's Will" and Its West European Sources]. Iur'ev, 1915.

Harnack, A. von. "Theodoret." *The Encyclopedia Britannica* 22 (1949): 58–59.

Harvanek, R. F. "Gregory of Nyssa, St." *New Catholic Encyclopedia* 6: 794–96.

Healy, P. J. "Valentinus and Valentinians." *The Catholic Encyclopedia* 15: 256.

Hobbes, Thomas. *Leviathan*. New York: Washington Square Press, 1964.

Hunter-Blair, D. O. "Gregory Nazianzus." *The Catholic Encyclopedia* 7: 10–15.

Kapterev, N. F. *Patriarkh Nikon i ego pretivniki v dielie ispravleniia tserkovnykh obriadov. Vremia patriarshestva Iosifa* [Patriarch Nikon and His Opponents in the Correction of Church Rites. The Patriarchate of Joseph]. 2d ed. Zagorsk (Sergiev posad), 1913.

———. *Patriarkh Nikon i Tsar' Aleksiei Mikhailovich* [Patriarch Nikon and Tsar Alexis Mikhailovich]. 2 vols. Zagorsk (Sergiev posad), 1910–12.

Karpovich, Michael. *Imperial Russia, 1801–1917*. New York: Holt, Rinehart and Winston, 1961.

Kartashev, A. V. "K voprosu o pravoslavii Feofana Prokopovicha" [On the Question of the Orthodoxy of Feofan Prokopovich]. *Sbornik statei v chest' Dmitriia Fomicha Kobeko ot sosluzhivtsev po Imperatorskoi Publichnoi bibliotekie* [A Collection of Articles in Honor of Dmitrii Fomich Kobeko From His Colleagues at the Imperial Public Library], pp. 225–36. St. Petersburg, 1913.

———. *Ocherki po istorii Russkoi Tserkvi.* [Essays on the History of the Russian Church]. 2 vols. Paris: YMCA Press, 1959.

Kedrov, N. I. *Dukhovnyi reglament v sviazi s preobrazovatel'noiu dieiatel'nost'iu Petra Velikago* [The Spiritual Regulation in Connection With the Reforming Activity of Peter the Great]. Moscow, 1886.

Kharlampovich, K. V. *Malorossiiskoe vliianie na velikorusskuiu tserkovnuiu zhizn'* [Little Russian Influence on Great Russian Church Life]. Vol. 1. 1914. Reprint. The Hague: Mouton, 1968.

Kirsch, J. P. "Leo I." *The Catholic Encyclopedia* 9: 154–57.

Kliuchevsky, V. O. *Sochineniia v vos'mi tomakh* [Works in Eight Volumes]. 8 vols. Moscow, 1956–59.

Konsky, M. "Prosvieshchennyi absolutizm." [Enlightened Absolutism]. *Entsiklopedicheskii slovar'* 49: 469–72.

Korkunov, N. M. *Russkoe gosudarstvennoe pravo* [Russian Public Law]. 2 vols. St. Petersburg, 1909.

Korolev, A. "Stefan Iavorsky." *Russkii biograficheskii slovar'* [The Russian Biographical Dictionary] 19:413–22. 25 vols. 1896–1918. Reprint. New York, 1962.

Kovalensky, M. N. *Proiskhozhdenie tsarskoi vlasti* [The Origin of Tsarist Authority]. Moscow, 1922.

K-v, V. "Vzgliad Nikona na znachenie patriarshei vlasti" [Nikon's View of the Meaning of Patriarchal Authority]. *Zhurnal Ministerstva na-rodnago prosvieshcheniia,* December 1880, pp. 233–67.

Lappo-Danilevsky, A. S. "Ideia gosudarstva i glavnieishie momenty eia razvitiia v Rossii so vremeni smuty i do epokhi preobrazovanii" [The Idea of the State and the Most Important Moments of Its Development From the Time of Troubles to the Period of Reforms]. *Golos minuvshago* [The Voice of the Past] 12 (1914): 5–38.

Lipski, Alexander. "A Re-examination of the Dark Era of Anna Ioannovna." *Slavic Review* 16 (1956):477–88.

McSorley, J. "Basil." *The Catholic Encyclopedia* 2: 330–34.

Makarii, metropolitan of Moscow. *Istoriia Russkoi Tserkvi* [History of the Russian Church]. 11 vols. St. Petersburg, 1857–82.

Medlin, William K. *Moscow and East Rome.* Geneva: Librairie E. Droz, 1952.

Miakotin, V. A. "Dukhovnyi reglament" [The Spiritual Regulation]. *Entsiklopedicheskii slovar'* 21: 273.

Miliukov, P. N. *Gosudarstvennoe khoziaistvo Rossii v pervoi chetverti XVIII stolietiia i reforma Petra Velikago* [The State Economy of Russia in the First Quarter of the Eighteenth Century and the Reform of Peter the Great]. 2d ed. St. Petersburg, 1905.

———. "Kollegii" [The Colleges]. *Entsiklopedicheskii slovar'* 30: 692–94.

———. *Ocherki po istorii russkoi kul'tury* [Essays on the History of Russian Culture]. 3 vols. Paris and The Hague, 1930–64.

Morris, James. *The World of Venice.* New York: Pantheon, 1960.

Morozov, P. "Feofan Prokopovich." *Entsiklopedicheskii slovar'* 82: 929–30.

———. "Feofan Prokopovich kak pisatel' " [Feofan Prokopovich as a Writer]. *Zhurnal Ministerstva narodnago prosvieshcheniia,* February 1880, pp. 416–76; March 1880, pp. 72–133; May 1880, pp. 107–48; June 1880, pp. 251–311; July 1880, pp. 1–49; August 1880, pp. 293–354; September 1880, pp. 1–65.

Mouravieff, A. N. *A History of the Church of Russia,* trans. R. W. Blackmore. London: J. H. Parker, 1842.

New Catholic Encyclopedia. 15 vols. New York: McGraw-Hill, 1967.

Nikol'sky, N. M. *Istoriia Russkoi Tserkvi* [History of the Russian Church]. Moscow, 1930.

———. "Tserkovnaia reforma Petra" [Peter's Church Reform]. In *Tri vieka* 3: 180–97.

Nosovich, I. "Vsep'ianieishii sobor, uchrezhdennyi Petrom Velikim" [The All-drunken Council Established by Peter the Great]. *Russkaia starina,* December 1874, pp. 734–39.

Obolensky, Dmitri. "Russia's Byzantine Heritage." In *Oxford Slavonic Papers* 1: 37–63. Edited by S. Konovalov. Oxford: Clarendon Press, 1950.

Oliva, Lawrence J. *Russia in the Era of Peter the Great.* Englewood Cliffs, N.J.: Prentice-Hall, 1969.

"O preobrazovanii vysshago tserkovnago upravleniia Petrom I" [On the Reform of the Highest Ecclesiastical Administration by Peter I]. *Russkii viestnik* [The Russian Messenger], November 1891, pp. 166–96.

Ostrogorsky, George. *History of the Byzantine State.* New Brunswick, N.J.: Rutgers University Press, 1957.

Palmer, William. *The Patriarch and the Tsar.* 6 vols. London: Trübner & Co., 1871–76.

Pal'mov, N. N. *Postrizhenie v monashestvo. Chiny postrizheniia v monashestvo v Grecheskoi Tserkvi* [Tonsure Into Monastic Life. The Rites of Tonsure Into Monastic Life in the Greek Church]. Kiev, 1914.

Parker, Thomas M. *Christianity and the State in the Light of History.* London: Adam and Charles Black, 1955

"Patriarkh Nikon po vnov' otkrytym N. A. Gibbenet materialam" [Patriarch Nikon in the Light of Material Recently Uncovered by N. A. Gibbenet]. *Russkaia starina,* August 1884, pp. 223–54.

Pattison, Mark. *Essays.* 2 vols. London: G. Routledge and Sons, 1889.

Pekarsky, P. P. *Nauka i literatura v Rossii pri Petrie Velikom* [Learning and Literature in Russia Under Peter the Great]. 2 vols. St. Petersburg, 1862.

Perfetsky, E. Iu. *Car Petr I i Leibnitz* [Tsar Peter I and Leibnitz]. Bratislava, 1925.

Platonov, S. F. *Petr Velikii, lichnost' i deiatel'nost'* [Peter the Great, Personality and Activity]. Leningrad, 1925 (?).

Podgursky, D. "De Auctoritate Sacro-Sanctae Synodi Rossicae." *Trudy Kievskoi dukhovnoi akademii,* October 1869, pp. 113–42.

"Polk." *Bol'shaia sovetskaia entsiklopediia* [The Large Soviet Encyclopedia] 33: 598–99. 2d ed. 51 vols. Moscow, 1949–58.

Poncelet, A. "Irenaeus." *The Catholic Encyclopedia* 8: 130–31.

Popov, V. "O sviatieishem sinodie i ob ustanovleniiakh pri nem v tsarstvovanie Petra I, 1721–1725" [On the Most Holy Synod and Its Institutions in the Reign of Peter I, 1721–1725]. *Zhurnal Ministerstva narodnago prosvieshcheniia,* February 1881, pp. 222–63; March 1881, pp. 1–51.

Portalié, E. "Augustine." *The Catholic Encyclopedia* 2:84–104.

"Postrizhenie" [Tonsure]. *Entsiklopedicheskii slovar'* 48: 712.

Pufendorf, Samuel von. *The Elements of Universal Jurisprudence,* trans.

W. A. Oldfather. Oxford: Clarendon Press; London: H. Milford, 1931.

————. *On the Law of Nature and Nations*. Translated by C. H. and W. A. Oldfather. Oxford: Clarendon Press; London: H. Milford, 1934.

Pypin, A. N. "Feofan Prokopovich i ego protivniki" [Feofan Prokopovich and His Opponents]. *Viestnik Evropy* 6 (1869):791–818.

"Reglament." *Iuridicheskii slovar'* [A Legal Dictionary] 2: 325–26. 2d ed. Moscow, 1956.

Riasanovsky, V. A. *Obzor russkoi kul'tury* [Historical Survey of Russian Culture]. 2 vols. in 3. Eugene, Ore.: V. A. Riasanovsky, 1947–48.

Rozhdestvensky, S. V. *Epokha preobrazovaniia Petra Velikago i russkaia shkola novago vremeni* [The Period of Peter the Great's Reform and the Russian School of Recent Time]. St. Petersburg, 1903.

Runkevich, S. G. *Arkhierei Petrovskoi epokhi v ikh perepiskie s Petrom Velikim* [Bishops of the Petrine Period in Their Correspondence With Peter the Great]. St. Petersburg, 1906.

————. *Istoriia Russkoi Tserkvi pod upravleniem Sviatieishago sinoda* [The History of the Russian Church Under the Administration of the Most Holy Synod]. Vol. 1 of *Uchrezhdenie i pervonachal'noe ustroistvo Sviatieishago pravitel'stvuiushchago sinoda, 1721–1725 gg.* [The Establishment and Initial Organization of the Most Holy Ruling Synod, 1721–1725]. St. Petersburg, 1900.

Russkaia starina [Russian Antiquity]. Monthly, 1870–1917; bimonthly, 1918.

Samarin, Iurii. *Stefan Iavorskii i Feofan Prokopovich* [Stefan Iavorsky and Feofan Prokopovich]. In *Sochineniia* [Works], vol. 5. Edited by D. Samarin. 10 vols. Moscow, 1877–96.

Schmemann, Alexander. *The Historical Road of Eastern Orthodoxy*. Translated by L. W. Kesich. New York: Holt, Rinehart and Winston, 1963.

Schuyler, Eugene. *Peter the Great, Emperor of Russia. A Study of Historical Biography*. 2 vols. New York: Charles Scribner's Sons, 1890.

Semevsky, M. I. *Slovo i dielo!* [Word and Deed!]. 3d ed. St. Petersburg, 1885.

Šerech, J. "Stefan Iavorski and the Conflict of Ideologies in the Age of Peter the Great." *Slavonic and East European Review* 30 (December 1951): 40–62.

Sergieevich, V. I. *Lektsii i izsliedovaniia po drevnei istorii russkago prava* [Lectures and Studies in the Early History of Russian Law]. St. Petersburg, 1910.

Shchegolev, P. E. "Stefan Iavorskii." *Entsiklopedicheskii slovar'* 62: 638–41.

Shmurlo, E. F. "Kriticheskiia zametki po istorii Petra Velikago" [Critical Notes on the History of Peter the Great] *Zhurnal Ministerstva narodnago prosvieshcheniia,* May 1900 pp. 54–95; August 1900, pp. 193–234; October 1900, pp. 335–66; December 1901, pp. 237–49; April 1902, pp. 421–39; June 1902, pp. 233–56.

———. "Petr Velikii v otsienkie sovremennikov i potomstva" [Peter the Great in the Estimation of Contemporaries and Posterity]. *Zhurnal Ministerstva narodnago prosviesheniia,* October 1911, pp. 315–40; November 1911, pp. 1–37; December 1911, pp. 201–73; May 1912, pp. 1–40; June 1912 pp. 193–259.

Shpakov, A. Ia. "Gosudarstvo i tserkov' v ikh vzaimnykh otnosheniiakh v Moskovskom gosudarstvie. Uchrezhdenie patriashestva v Rossii" [State and Church in Their Mutual Relations in the Muscovite State. The Formation of the Patriarchate in Russia]. In *Zapiski Imperatorskago Novorossiiskago universiteta Iuridicheskago fakul'teta* [Transactions of the Law Faculty of the Imperial University of Novorossiisk], vol. 6. Odessa, 1912.

"Shutki i potiekhi Petra Velikago. Sobstvennoruchno im napisannye chiny izbraniia i postavleniia kniaz'-papy, shutochnyia poslaniia, ukazy, rospisi i podpiski 1690–1725 gg." [Peter the Great's Jokes and Games. The Rites of Election and Installation of the Prince-Pope, Jocose Letters, Ukases, Assignments, and Signatures Written in His Own Hand, 1690–1725]. *Russkaia starina,* June 1872, pp. 845–92.

Sinker, R. "Stephen, St." In *A Dictionary of Christian Antiquities,* ed. Sir W. Smith and S. Cheetham, 2:1929–33. London, 1893.

Slitsan, B. G. "Reforma tserkovnogo upravleniia" [The Reform of the Church Administration]. In *Ocherki istorii SSSR. Rossiia v pervoi chetverti XVIII v.* [Essays on the History of the USSR. Russia in the First Quarter of the Eighteenth Century], ed. B. B. Kafengauz and N. I. Pavlenko, pp. 371–81. Moscow, 1954.

Slutsky, S. S., trans. "Petr Velikii i papstvo. Iz putevykh zapisok Avgusta Kotsebu" [Peter the Great and the Papacy. From the Travel Notes of August Kotzebue]. *Russkii arkhiv* [Russian Archives] 11 (1903): 392–98.

Smirnov, N. A., ed. "Tserkov' i russkii absoliutizm v XVIII v." [The Church and Russian Absolutism in the Eighteenth Century]. In *Tserkov' v istorii Rossii (IX v.-1917 g.)* [The Church in Russian History (From the Ninth Century to 1917)]. pp. 162–205. Moscow, 1967.

Smith, Preserved. *Origins of Modern Culture, 1543–1687.* New York: Collier Books, 1962.

Smolitsch, Igor. *Geschichte der russischen Kirche 1700–1917.* Leiden: E. J. Brill, 1964.

Bibliography

————. *Russisches Mönchtum.* Würzburg: Augustinus-Verlag, 1953.

"Starodub." *Bol'shaia sovetskaia entsiklopediia* [The Large Soviet Encyclopedia] 40: 507. 2d ed. 51 vols. Moscow, 1949–58.

Stupperich, R. "Feofan Prokopovič und Johann Buddeus." *Zeitschrift für osteuropäische Geschichte* 9, no. 5:341–62. 1935. Reprint. Graz, 1966.

Sumner, B. H. *Peter the Great and the Emergence of Russia.* London: English Universities Press, 1960.

Syromiatnikov, B. I. *"Reguliarnoe" gosudarstvo Petra I i ego ideologiia* [The "Regular" State of Peter I and Its Ideology]. Moscow, 1943.

Szeftel, Marc. "Russian Government Before 1905–06." In *Essays in Russian and Soviet History in Honor of Geroid Tanquary Robinson,* ed. J. Curtiss, pp. 105–19. New York: Columbia University Press, 1963.

Temnikovsky, E. N. *Odin iz istochnikov Dukhovnago reglamenta* [One of the Sources of the Spiritual Regulation]. Khar'kov, 1909.

————. *Polozhenie Imperatora vserossiiskago v Russkoi Pravoslavnoi Tserkvi v sviazi s obshchim ucheniem o tserkovnoi vlasti* [The Position of the All-Russian Emperor in the Russian Orthodox Church in Connection With the Common Teaching Concerning Ecclesiastical Authority]. Iaroslavl', 1909.

Ternovsky, F. "Imperator Petr I v ego otnosheniiakh k katolichestvu i protestantstvu" [Emperor Peter I in His Relations With Catholicism and Protestantism]. *Trudy Kievskoi dukhovnoi akademii,* March 1869, pp. 373–404.

————. "M. Stefan Iavorskii" [Metropolitan Stefan Iavorsky]. *Trudy Kievskoi dukhovnoi akademii,* January 1864, pp. 36–70; March 1864, pp. 237–90; June 1864, pp. 137–86.

Tikhomirov, M. N. *Istochnikovedenie istorii SSSR* [A Study of the Sources for the History of the USSR], vol. 1. Moscow, 1962.

Titlinov, B. "Feofan Prokopovich." In *Russkii biograficheskii slovar'* [The Russian Biographical Dictionary] 25:399–448. Reprint. New York, 1962.

Tri vieka [Three Centuries]. Edited by V. V. Kallash. 6 vols. St. Petersburg, 1912.

"Tserkvi domovyia" [Household Churches]. *Entsiklopedicheskii slovar'* 75: 62.

Ulanov, V. Ia. "Oppozitsiia Petru Velikomu" [Opposition to Peter the Great]. In *Tri vieka* 3: 58–86.

————. "Preobrazovanie upravleniia pri Petrie Velikom" [Administrative Reform Under Peter the Great]. In *Tri vieka* 3: 220–39.

Ustrialov, N. G. *Istoriia tsarstvovaniia Petra Velikago* [History of the Reign of Peter the Great]. 5 vols. St. Petersburg, 1858–63.

Vasiliev, A. A. *History of the Byzantine Empire.* 2 vols. Madison: University of Wisconsin Press, 1958.

Venturi, Franco. "Feofan Prokopovič." *Annali aelle Facoltà di Lettere, Filosofia e Magistero dell' Università di Cagliari* 21, no. 1 (1953): 625–80.

Verkhovskoi, P. V. *K voprosu o "fal'sifikatsii" Dukhovnago reglamenta* [On the Question of the "Falsification" of the Spiritual Regulation]. Petrograd, 1914.

————. *Ocherki po istorii Russkoi Tserkvi v XVIII i XIX st.* [Essays on the History of the Russian Church in the Eighteenth and Nineteenth Centuries]. Warsaw, 1912.

————. *Uchrezhdenie Dukhovnoi kollegii i Dukhovnyi reglament. K voprosu ob otnoshenii Tserkvi i gosudarstva v Rossii* [The Establishment of the Spiritual College and the Spiritual Regulation. On the Question of the Relations of Church and State in Russia]. 2 vols. Rostov-on-the-Don, 1916.

Veselovsky, N. I. "Patriarshiia votchiny v Rossii" [Patriarchal Landed Estates in Russia]. *Entsiklopedicheskii slovar'* 45: 33–36.

Vishnevsky, D. *Kievskaia akademiia v pervoi polovinie XVIII stolietiia* [The Kiev Academy in the First Half of the Eighteenth Century]. Kiev, 1903.

Vladimirsky-Budanov, M. F. "Gosudarstvo i narodnoe obrazovanie v Rossii s XVII vieka do uchrezhdeniia ministerstv" [The State and Public Education in Russia From the Seventeenth Century to the Formation of Ministries]. *Zhurnal Ministerstva narodnago prosvieshcheniia,* October 1873, pp. 165–220; November 1873, pp. 36–70; April 1874, pp. 246–77; May 1874, pp. 136–57. Published separately as *Gosudarstvo i narodnoe obrazovanie v Rossii XVIII-go vieka* [The State and Public Education in Russia of the Eighteenth Century]. Iaroslavl', 1874.

————. *Obzor istorii russkago prava* [Survey of the History of Russian Law]. 6th ed. Kiev, 1909.

Weber, N. A. "Cathari." *The Catholic Encyclopedia* 3: 435–37.

Wittram, Reinhard. *Peter I, Czar und Kaiser.* 2 vols. Göttingen: Vandenhoeck & Ruprecht, 1964.

Zabielin, I. "O dietstvie Petra Velikago' [On Peter the Great's Childhood]. *Arkhiv istoriko-iuridicheskikh sviedienii otnosiashchikhsia do Rossii* [Archives of Historical and Judicial Information on Russia], ed. N. Kalachov, 3:139–80. St. Petersburg and Moscow, 1861.

Zernov, N. "Peter the Great and the Establishment of the Russian Church." *The Church Quarterly Review* 125, no. 250 (January–March 1938):265–93.

Zharinov, D. A. "Petr Velikii kak zakonodatel' i 'Pravda voli monarshei'" [Peter the Great as Legislator and "The Justice of the Monarch's Will"]. In *Tri vieka* 3: 163–79.

"Zhitie sviatieishago Patriarkha Nikona, pisannoe niekotorym byvshim pri nem klirikom" [The Life of His Eminence, Patriarch Nikon, Written by a Contemporary Cleric]. *Russkii arkhiv* [Russian Archives] 3 (1909): 1–110.

Zhordaniia, F. *Sviatieishii sinod pri Petrie Velikom v ego otnoshenii k Pravitel'stvuiushchemu senatu* [The Most Holy Synod Under Peter the Great in Its Relationship to the Ruling Senate]. Tiflis, 1882.

Zhurnal Ministerstva narodnago prosvieshcheniia [Journal of the Ministry of Public Education]. 590 nos. in 246 vols. St. Petersburg, Petrograd, 1834–1917.

Zinchenko, I. K. "O nashem vysshem tserkovnom upravlenii" [On Our Higher Ecclesiastical Administration]. *Russkii viestnik* [The Russian Messenger], April 1891, pp. 4–42.

Znamensky, P. V. *Dukhovnyia shkoly v Rossii do reformy 1808 goda* [Ecclesiastical Schools in Russia to the Reform of 1808]. Kazan', 1881.

———. *Prikhodskoe dukhovenstvo v Rossii so vremeni reformy Petra* [Parish Clergy in Russia From the Time of Peter's Reform]. Kazan', 1873.

Index

Aaron, bishop of Karelia: signatory to *Spiritual Regulation,* 114n100

Academy: project for, 33-39; and Seminary, 39-43; graduates to enter state service, 113n79

Act of Supremacy (1534), xxxvii

Adrian, patriarch of Moscow, xxii

Afanasii, archbishop of Kholmogory. *See* Liubimov, Afanasii

Afanasii, hegumen of Tolgsky Monastery. *See* Kontoeidēs, Anastasios

Africa, 36

Alexander Nevsky Monastery: Spiritual College meeting at, 104n5; Feodosii Ianovsky, archimandrite of, 114n100, 120n151

Alexis (1629-76), tsar: encroachments on church jurisdiction, xvi; issue of chanting in many parts, 108n26

Alexis (1690-1718), tsarevich: education of, xxxv; removed from succession, 100n140; focal point of reaction, 115-16n111

Alleluia controversy, 13-14; in Pskov, 105-6n16

Almsgiving: abused, 54; system for, 55

Altar-breads (*prosfory*), 107n21

America, 36

Anathema. *See* Excommunication

Anne empress (1730-40), 109n33

Anne queen of Great Britain and Ireland, 98n129

Anthony the Great, Saint, 80, 112n143

Antonii, archimandrite of Moscow Zlatoustov Monastery: signatory to *Spiritual Regulation,* 114n100

Apraksin, Fedor Matveevich (1661-1728), admiral, graf, senator: signatory to *Spiritual Regulation,* 114n100

Areopagites, 8

Arians, 34, 111n62

Aristenos, Alexis, canonist, 65, 117n122

Arius 31, 111n62

Army, Russian: expenditures for, xxi-xxii; in war with Sweden, xxvi; reformed by Peter, 30; bishops' permission required

Sanhedrin, 8-9

Schismatics (*raskol'niki*). *See* Old Believers

Schmemann, Alexander, ix, xxxvii

Scholasticism, Protestant, x

Schools, episcopal, 20-21; for ordination, 58; for ecclesiastical careers, 112n79

Secrecy: sworn requirement for, 6

"Secularization of the church," xv, 91n32

Seminary: project for, 39-43; graduates to enter state service, 113n79

Senate, Ruling (*Pravitel'stvuiushchii Senat*), 12, 87n2, 96n87, 104n6, 113n93; jurisdiction over cases involving injury to ecclesiastics, 53; to consider tax for support of priesthood, 55; approves *Spiritual Regulation*, 56; is sent copy of *Spiritual Regulation* by Synod, 89n3; summons recalcitrant bishops, 90n12

Serving people (*sluzhilye liudi*), xxii; in Manifesto, 3. *See also* Gentry

Shafirov, Peter Pavlovich, baron, senator: signatory to *Spiritual Regulation*, 114n100

Sil'vestr, metropolitan of Smolensk: signatory to *Spiritual Regulation*, 114n100

Simeonov, Ioann, protopresbyter of the Trinity Cathedral in St. Petersburg, original member (assessor) of Synod: signatory to oath, 104n5; to first final draft and first printed edition of Supplement, 119n149; to second printed edition of Supplement, 121n152

Smielich, Peter, archimandrite of the Moscow Simonov Monastery, original member (councilor) of Synod: signatory to oath, 104n5; to *Spiritual Regulation*, 114n100; to first final draft and first printed edition of Supplement, 119n149; to second final draft and second printed edition of Supplement, 120n151

Smith, Preserved, xxxv

Sophia, Peter's half sister and regent, 93

Spiritual Regulation, xv, xxv, 7, 85-86n1, 94n71, 95n73, 96n97, 100n138, 102n3, 103n5, 105-n13, 109n32, 113n93, 94, 116n112; signed by Peter, ix, 56, 114n100, 115n101, 102, 110; secular character of, x; compulsion upon clergy to sign, xi; effect upon church administration, xii; and reference to patriarchal authority, xvii; implementation facilitated by Nikonian reform, xix; emerges from earlier Petrine legislation, xxiii; not all objectives realized, xxiv; related to regulations governing other reforms, xxviii, 30; origin of, xxxi; entrusted to Prokopovich, xxxii; and Pufendorf, xxxv; related to *Kirchenordnungen*, xxxvi; as "program for a Russian Reformation," xxxvii; significance of, xxxviii; in Manifesto, 3-4; in oath, 5; in Supplement, 57, 59, 84; to be copied by candidates for priesthood, 59; publication of, 87-89n3; signatories to, 114-15n100

Squallers (*klikushi*), 20, 109n33

Starodub district, 14, 107n23

State expenditures, xxvi; for mili-